LORD

Can Do

*Snapshots of His Goodness
and Grace*

Sharon Sekerak

ISBN 978-1-0980-0654-9 (paperback)
ISBN 978-1-0980-0655-6 (digital)

Christian Faith Publishing, Inc.
832 Park Avenue
Meadville, PA 16335
www.christianfaithpublishing.com

Printed in the United States of America

I want to thank the following people, each of whom played a unique and vital role in the creation of this book.

Carol: my oldest friend and first writing partner.
Eben: God used you to make me step out and give voice to my desire to write.
Rick: you not only took time away from your own work to read mine, you provided the encouragement I needed to keep at it.
Dale: you were the mind behind "The Field" and "Not This One". It was fun working with you to bring them to life. Keep the ideas coming!
Ben and Sarah: I am grateful to you, my editors and teachers.
My dear family: thank you for putting up with me as I grow, albeit ever so slowly, in Christ.

Contents

Introduction

Y ou are not "holding" this book because you loved the title or the artwork, although that may be true. I believe you are reading these words because this book contains something specifically for you. I don't say that because I think I am a fount of knowledge or because I think I'm such a gifted writer. I just don't believe in coincidences. I believe you are looking at this book because God has something tucked away inside it just for you. If you are feeling resistant to that idea, that's okay. You can always set this book aside and walk away. If it's for you, you'll be drawn back to it.

I have been writing since I was thirteen. At first, my best friend and I wrote without a plan or thought. One of us would write a few paragraphs and pass it to the other just to see how she would move the story forward. It was great fun but, as you can imagine, not very productive. We spent a lot of time doing the enjoyable part: planning the story. We ended up with lots of individual scenes, which were basically worthless because they hadn't been connected cohesively. That part of writing is, I learned, a lot harder than it sounds. Consequently, once I got married and had children, I pretty much abandoned my dream of writing.

Fast-forward approximately forty years, during which time I had come into a serious relationship with Jesus Christ. When the desire to write began to resurface, I remembered two short stories I had started years earlier. It occurred to me that both could be used to point to God's goodness and power, which was what I longed to do. However, I knew I would have to modify both stories to suit that purpose, and I was unskilled in the art of writing. To my surprise, when I reread them, they were better than I remembered. I got an inkling that while I didn't yet have the expertise to write a multifaceted novel, I might be able to write something shorter with God's help.

While I tinkered with those short stories, I also returned to a thought that had been with me for quite some time. Who said it even had to be a short story? Perhaps someone might be encouraged by things the Lord has shown me and by what he has done in me and around me over the years.

As the title suggests, what follows is not a single story but rather a collection of snapshots.

To ease what might otherwise be jarring transitions between them, I have organized these pieces into sections. Although there is some overlap, part one is primarily aspects of my testimony. Parts two and three both contain lessons God has taught me. However, unlike part two, the lessons in the third section started as sparks in my imagination. I believe the Holy Spirit gave me these images and I hope that I have fleshed them out according to his vision for them.

My desire is that you see the Lord's kindness and strength, his gentle leading, and even his humor through my experiences. More importantly, I pray that if you haven't already, you will begin to notice his hand in your own life.

PART 1

Joy Comes In the Morning

Perhaps the best place to start is with the story of my own path to saving faith. You will see bits of that journey throughout this book, and having this background may give those stories more depth. I feel compelled to acknowledge that this account represents only my perspective. My family would undoubtedly report these events differently. Moreover, even though what I have recorded here is the way I perceived things to be at the time, I have learned a great deal about myself since.

My father hated religion. It was his opinion that the church was full of hypocrites and only wanted your money. My mother tried to give us spirituality, but because she wasn't raised around any Christians, her theology was often incorrect. As a result, even though I have believed in God for as long as I can remember, mine was what you might call a "Designer God." You know, where a person takes a little of this and a little of that and calls it God. Reincarnation made sense to me, as did the idea that God is actually in every part of creation. Back then, I was sure that hugging a tree was akin to hugging God.

I knew about Jesus. I knew about him in the same way I knew about Abraham Lincoln. I was convinced that he was the Son of God. However, looking back, it's plain that I didn't comprehend sin and redemption. I saw him as the savior, but I found it hard to believe that he walked on water or raised people from the dead.

What *was* all too real to me was the colossal hole in my heart! I may not have understood salvation, but I hungered for Jesus and invited him into my life three times in my teens and early twenties. I joined a church. I even got baptized twice, but that hole was always still there. As a result, my view for years was that while God maintained the universe, I needed to manage my own world.

As much as I longed to feel God's love, I didn't seem able to get close to him. Eventually, I concluded that either he was a distant God or, more likely, something was wrong with me. Consequently, I lived with chronic, low-level depression for years. I remember walking around at my first job trying to comfort myself by repeating, "God is in his heaven, and all is right with the world." I believed what I was saying, but it did nothing to alleviate my discomfort. What I now understand is that, as is the case with most platitudes, this statement seemed like something that *should* fix everything (if only I could get it through my head). However, upon closer inspection, neither half of that mantra is entirely true. The first part suggests a distant God who is sitting off in heaven somewhere, while the second half denies what a mess the world really is.

During that season of life, I often had two demonic dreams. I believe they were related and that together they established a demonic stronghold that I sometimes still struggle with today.

The first dream always opened with me finding myself in the same pitch-black cave. Because I'd had the dream so many times, I knew immediately that something grotesque was in there with me. Even though I couldn't see it, I could sense it drawing steadily closer. I was hideously aware that it intended to devour me. As is the way with dreams, I knew that it wanted more than my mere flesh and that the devouring would go on forever. Anxiety had morphed into a blind panic by the time a soft voice whispered soothingly, "Be still. If your faith is strong enough, it won't be able to get you." I believed that gentle voice spoke the truth. So time after time, I tried to summon the level of faith necessary to keep the evil horror at bay. I always woke up just as the thing reached me.

Back then, I thought that soft voice was God's. I believed that he was hoping *this* time I would have enough faith to save myself. For such a long time, I lived with a sense of failure. Every dream added to the shame I felt for having let my God down—yet again.

In the second dream, I could hear someone I dearly loved being torn apart in the basement. My stomach churned listening to their terrified screams and the roars made by whatever it was that had them. I desperately wanted to go down to help, but I could never get past my fear. Again and again, I just stood there frozen, listening to them begging for my help until it was over, and they finally fell silent.

I have no doubt that the devil's intention was to undermine my faith through these dreams. His first move was to convince me that it was God rather than him telling me that I had the ability to save myself. He used the dreams to constantly reinforce what he wanted me to believe: God isn't who you think he is. He can't (or won't) rescue you. You are on your own. You aren't able to get close to him because you are weak and grossly self-centered. To this day, I occasionally battle the fear that God will ask me to sacrifice myself in some way, and I will let him down.

After I accepted Christ, I couldn't understand why God would allow Satan so much access to my mind and emotions when I was so young and inexperienced. I also wondered why he would leave me in that wilderness for thirty-five years. Jesus knew I wanted him, and that my strange theology was not willful. I never presumed to scold God, but I did speculate about why he didn't send me to a good church years earlier, one that would put me on the right track.

I won't know for sure how everything fits together until I get to heaven. Nevertheless, I believe God used these dreams to teach me something about how Satan operates, in part so that I would be better equipped to help others recognize his tactics in the future.

I met my future husband when I was twenty-three. We dated for two and a half years before he asked me to marry him. When that day finally came, I felt torn. I wanted to grow old with this wonderful man, but I also had reservations:

He didn't appear to need anyone (I love feeling needed). He was disdainful of strong emotions (I am a person who feels things deeply). He was neither affectionate nor playful (laughter and touch are vital to me). Nevertheless, because I was young and in love, I convinced myself that he would change after we got married in October 1978.

As you can imagine, our first few years together were rather rocky. We both had our issues, but my expectations of marriage were unhealthy and unreasonable. In my naivety, I expected my husband to fill that cavernous hole in my heart. I reasoned, cried, and finally demanded the attention I craved. Unfortunately, all of that emotion only pushed him away and shut him down. The poor man was so overwhelmed by my attempts to "help" him understand my point of view that he often fell asleep while I was baring my heart to him (for the 400th time). I couldn't see our sick dance. It looked to me as if he didn't really care about me.

One night, exasperated by his yawning, I stormed out of our bedroom to sleep on the couch. To me, his apparent exhaustion was nothing more than a passive-aggressive way of telling me he didn't care about what I was saying. I sat there agonizing over the sorry state of our marriage, yearning like a schoolgirl for him to come and make things right—that is, until I heard him snoring! In a heartbeat, I felt my face grow hot with rage. Unbidden images of myself sneaking into our bedroom, baseball bat in hand, and beating the living snot out of him rolled across my mind.

At the time, I blamed my dear husband for most of our problems. I often asked God what was wrong with him. Beneath that question, however, lurked a profound and long-standing doubt. After all, his distance and increasingly negative reaction to my emotional needs only reinforced what I'd heard most of my life. *You want too much. You are too emotional.* The creeping fear was that there actually was something wrong with me and that I was unloved because I was, at heart, unlovable.

Things got easier for a while once our children came along because I had someone else to focus on. Having little ones who needed me took a lot of pressure off my husband. A part of me knew that it wasn't healthy to invest most of my love and attention in my children, but it provided the relief that my husband and I both needed at the time.

Looking back, it felt like God was kind of on the sidelines. I prayed whenever things got too hard, but the rest of the time, I did whatever felt right in my own eyes. I honestly didn't know it could be any other way. Over the next four-teen years, this ineffective approach to life did nothing to slow the steady deterioration of my relationship with my daughter. Neither did the fact that my husband was neither able nor willing to be around our constant drama. My child's tre-mendous pain and anger, as well as my unhealthy response to them, sent him to the garage every time. I constantly struggled with my inability to improve our relationship, and I could not control the impact our negative interactions were having on our family.

I began hearing God's call to me through a *tremendous* hunger for peace. I saw what I wanted in two people at work. They responded to life's challenges differently than anyone else. Although we never talked about it, I knew they were Christians. It was evident to me that their faith was the reason they were generally positive, calm, and peaceful.

I don't remember how it came about, but it was during this season that I began reading the *Left Behind* series by Tim LaHaye and Jerry B. Jenkins. Even though these books present only one of several interpretation of the end times, God used them powerfully in my life. Having had no Christian teaching, I was genuinely surprised to learn that you don't get to heaven by being good!

The image of the tribulation painted by the authors scared me. I most definitely did *not* want to be one of the people still left on earth after God lifts his hand of blessing and protection from it. I wanted to spend eternity with Jesus. Obviously, God was fitting together the pieces, sovereignly preparing me for what came next.

The most painful phase of God's plan for my salvation began when my son went away to college. I love my daughter more than I can say, but by that time it often felt as if she viewed me as her enemy. All we did was clash—all the time—about everything. At the same time, my son who had typically been easy-going was preparing to move out. I felt as if I had failed one child miserably, and the other one was slipping out of my life. In addition, was the sense that my husband and I were operating more like business partners than husband and wife. I was miserable!

I knew my son's leaving was healthy and right, and I did my best not to make him responsible for my feelings. Nevertheless, watching my younger child walk away from me on his first day at college felt like having open-heart surgery without anesthesia. I am quite aware of how dramatic that sounds, but honestly, at that moment, all I could see in front of me were loneliness and useless old age.

Once we got back home, things settled into a new normal. I shook my head at the intensity of that experience and breathed a sigh of relief because I felt confident I had put all of that insanity behind me. Unfortunately, that was not the case. It was so hard to see my son leave after every visit that a secret part of me couldn't even look forward to his coming home.

Every year, as he prepared to return to campus, my anxiety and depression started earlier in the summer and seemed to be harder to work through. By his junior year, dread settled on me on the fifth of July! I was thoroughly disgusted with myself. What I was experiencing was downright irrational. Nobody around me seemed to be especially bothered by his leaving. In fact, I couldn't find anyone else who had gone through this much angst when their child left home. I tried reasoning with myself: *You've been through this twice already, and you know things will settle down once he's gone. After all, he is only two hours away and he comes home regularly. For heaven's sake, he isn't even leaving for seven weeks!*

There was nothing logical about the whole situation. It scared me that I couldn't find joy in any of the things I used to love. I was secretly afraid that I might be having a breakdown. I did a lot of reaching out and soon learned that nobody understood what I was feeling, and that included me. It became abundantly clear that nobody could help me. To the contrary, people were beginning to get impatient with my inability to just pull myself together.

One morning as I stood folding laundry, I experienced a vision. I had the sense of myself standing on the edge of an abyss. Looking down, I saw my toes curled over the edge of the rocks. In an instant, I became aware of how much energy I had been expending in keeping my balance day after day and of how exhausted I had become. With that came the fear that eventually one of these cyclones of emotion would drive me over the edge. Nearly frantic, I looked around, hoping to find someone or something to grab onto, but there was nothing in sight. The vision ended leaving me back on solid ground physically, but more afraid than ever.

Despair and fear were my constant companions during that time, but every once in a while, something absolutely *amazing* would happen. Without warning, the oppressive cloud would lift. Hope returned, and I would get a sense that the future wasn't something to dread. The relief never lasted more than a minute or so, but even that temporary respite was phenomenal. God knew what it would take to bring me to the place I needed to be. While they were happening, those inexplicable periods of relief were glorious, but I still had only a limited view of the bigger picture. Looking back, I am certain that through those moments, our merciful Father was whispering to me, "Hold on, little one. Something good is coming. I promise."

My first inkling that God cared about my plight occurred while I was standing at the copier at work. Someone else's print came out before mine. The gigantic title "A Memo from God" caught my eye, so I read God's memo, which said in part, "Turn your roller coaster emotions over to me. I can and will take care of the things that are hurting you if you will just trust me." This was no coincidence! I was certain that God had given me a gift, something for me to cling to. I carried his memo around and read it whenever I began to feel overwhelmed, which was a *lot*. It always calmed the storm just enough to get me through.

Things came to a head on a Friday in July 2006. I had spent the day at a car show with my husband and two of his friends. I felt like I was walking around inside a *Twilight Zone* episode. Everyone around me seemed to be smiling. They were talking about paint jobs, engines and exhaust systems. People were happily eating hot dogs and drinking beer. Meanwhile, I felt like I was struggling just to keep my head above water. I had never felt so alone in my life.

On our way home, my husband wanted to stop at the drugstore. Something happened inside of me when he got out of our truck. Seeing my life partner walking away, happily absorbed in himself and entirely unaware of my turmoil, created an almost unfathomable desperation in me. You've heard about crying out to God? That is precisely what I did. I literally shouted, "I can't bear this! Please help me. Tell me what to do. I will do *anything*!"

There was no voice from heaven. My husband got back into the truck, and we went home, but my answer was on its way. The next day, my sister said she had found a church she liked and suggested I go with her. I attended Vineyard Christian Fellowship for the first time in July 2006. I don't remember much about the sermon because I was preoccupied with the image projected on the screen: a man on the beach, head thrown back, arms spread wide, abandoned to worship. Oh, how I wanted to do that! Instead, there I stood, arms wrapped around myself, afraid that if I opened myself up like that, my insides would all spill out.

When the pastor invited people to come forward for ministry and prayer time, I think I may have trampled several small children to get up there. As I stood there receiving prayer, Jesus helped me to let go. I wasn't even aware of doing it, but by the time I left the church that morning, I had somehow turned everything and everyone in my life over to him.

At first, all I felt was relief, but as that day progressed, I started to feel lighter. Not long into a walk with my dog, I realized that for the first time in ages, I was able to take a really deep breath. Looking up, I marveled at the sight of a flock of birds and the sky's astonishing shade of blue behind them. *Clearly, something had changed!*

God fashions unique experiences for each of us according to our need. Obviously, what I went through during those arduous years wasn't really about my son leaving home, or about my turbulent relationship with my husband and daughter. It was all about what Jesus said in Matthew 5:3, *"Blessed are the poor in spirit, for theirs is the kingdom of heaven."*

God had given me the horrible/wonderful gift of experiencing my true state without him so that I would cling to him more tightly once he rescued me. He gave me a glimpse into the abyss of living life on my own. And he made it abundantly clear that nothing on this earth is capable of saving me. Then, when I was ready—he came for me!

Jesus is 'the stone you builders rejected, which has become the cornerstone.' Salvation is found in no one else, for there is no other name under heaven given to mankind by which we must be saved." Acts 4:11–12

Whoever believes in him is not condemned, but whoever does not believe stands condemned already because they have not believed in the name of God's one and only Son. John 3:18

For the wages of sin is death, but the gift of God is eternal life in Christ Jesus our Lord. Romans 6:23

For it is by grace you have been saved, through faith—and this is not from yourselves, it is the gift of God—not by works, so that no one can boast. Ephesians 2:8–9

What Do You See When You Look at Me?

Lord, my head and my heart are at odds. Intellectually, I believe you love me apart from anything I do. Nevertheless, my heart persists in the thought that you are working in me *mainly* because you want to use me to further your kingdom. Father, I guess I don't really believe that I am truly loveable. Please tell me what you see when you look at me

The following is what I believe Father God said to me in response to my plea for truth. My prayer is that you would hear whatever he would say to you through his response to me and that you would be encouraged to ask him to reveal his heart for you.

My child, trust in my Word. I knew and loved you before I knitted you in your mother's womb. I set you apart at my very first thought to create you. You are indeed fearfully and wonderfully made (Psalm 139:14). However, dear one, you have a spiritual enemy. He works tirelessly to crush the heart of every little girl, robbing her of the ability to see what a beautiful creation she is. He has countless minions eager to do his vile bidding, but he takes particular delight in inflicting his damage through trusted people: friends, neighbors, teachers and, sadly, even family.

Daughter, I heard you say, with superb little girl glee, "Look at how pretty I am!" How disappointed I was to see the innocent delight in your eyes slowly extinguished as people in your life reprimanded you for voicing that simple truth. *I declare you—delightful!*

I rejoice in the lovely, tender heart I made especially for you. I intend it to bless those around you. However, the world disdains what it views as weakness. Seeing your yearning for intimacy and your ready tears, the world quickly branded you "too needy and emotional." Ah, but gentle one, it takes more courage to be open and compassionate than it does to be what the world calls strong. *I declare you—courageously tenderhearted, a vehicle for my healing touch!*

I created you to be outgoing, confident, and just a little bit sassy. With gentle guidance, those traits, along with the sensitivity I also gave you, would have yielded the leader I ordained. Unfortunately, those around you weren't able to see the potential in these sometimes frustrating traits. So rather than helping you smooth out the rough edges, they thoughtlessly branded you a "big mouth." Needing to please, you tried to change. Naturally, since I made those attributes integral to your personality, they continued to surface. Without patient shaping, your strength and outspokenness morphed into bossiness, which yielded still more negative feedback. Confused, you started withdrawing from people, thereby warping my original gifts even further. *I declare you—gracefully strong and outgoing!*

Because I create my children to be in relationship with each other, I delighted in your early openness. Your willingness to share yourself was wholly pure and right. How it pained me to watch you erect defenses against the wounds an uncaring, self-absorbed world inflicts on the innocent. *I declare you—blessedly childlike!*

Because I endow each of my children with thoughtful care, it was painful to see your body become a source of confusion and shame. It infuriated me to see your innocence stolen at such a tender age. I hated that his sin twisted not only your sexuality but also your opinion of how men view women. *I declare you—pure, lovely and eminently worthy of love and affection!*

I gave you a sturdy, courageous, steadfast little heart. My design would have had the adults in your life make you feel safe and secure so that you would find venturing into the unknown exciting rather than threatening. However, this is a broken world, and your enemy knew how to exploit the weaknesses of your caregivers and thereby lock you in a prison of anxiety. *I declare you free to "step off that cliff"—confident that I will catch you and that we will soar together in joyful abandon!*

I grieved the day you began to accept the wicked one's lie that you are somehow profoundly flawed and therefore unworthy of the love I created you to desire. On that day, you took shame as your identity. Hear me, dear heart: that is not the name I have for you, and it will *not* stand!

Beloved, you ask me what I see when I look at you. I see the trusting infant, the curious toddler, the openly loving child, and the increasingly guarded but still seeking teenager. I see the hopeful bride, and the naïve young mother determined to surround *her* children with health, love and truth. I can't help but see the achingly lonely middle-aged woman who realized that her children were leaving home as damaged as all of the others. I also see that magnificent moment when you cried out to me, and I introduced you to My Son.

Nevertheless, through *all* of those moments, I never lost sight of the singularly beautiful woman I created you to be. How I delight in calling her forth as you allow me to heal and restore you. *I declare you—my treasured creation, beloved by me for the woman you have* always *been in my sight.*

Then God said, "Let us make mankind in our image, in our likeness, so that they may rule over the fish in the sea and the birds in the sky, over the livestock and all the wild animals, and over all the creatures that move along the ground."

For you created my inmost being; you knit me together in my mother's womb. I praise you because I am fearfully and wonderfully made; your works are wonderful, I know that full well.

My frame was not hidden from you when I was made in the secret place, when I was woven together in the depths of the earth. Your eyes saw my unformed body; all the days ordained for me were written in your book before one of them came to be. Psalm 139:13–16

Can a mother forget the baby at her breast and have no compassion on the child she has borne? Though she may forget, I will not forget you! See, I have engraved you on the palms of my hands; your walls are ever before me. Isaiah 49:15–16

The LORD your God is with you, the Mighty Warrior who saves. He will take great delight in you; in his love he will no longer rebuke you, but will rejoice over you with singing. Zephaniah 3:17

The Way to Him

This poem is my attempt to capture what might have been happening in the spiritual realm during my difficult conversion experience. As previously stated, I had given my life to Christ more than once in my youth. I have no idea why, even though I sincerely wanted him, that hole in my heart always remained. However, I do know that through what I experienced during those years, he brought me to a place where I am positive that there is no savior other than Jesus.

Through seasons spent in deepest night,
He hid his face, that loving teacher.
My desperate clutching for
earthly hands too weak
Brought tears to holy eyes.
Yet steadfast he remained, looking
to the still greater good.
He whispered words of reassurance,
though my flesh perceived them not.

You're unaware, dear one, for
ready you must come.
But my hold on you is sure.
The abyss I keep at bay.

Finally, on that horrible/wonderful
day, broken at last and ready,
I cried out in desperation, as he knew I would.
"Help me, Father! I can endure no more!"
Heaven rejoiced, and God's decree was swift:
Fly, Spirit, bind up her heart and
instill glad hope anew.
Send the messenger and prepare her welcome.

Then God bent close and
whispered near my ear:
"The morning dawns, my precious
child. His name is Jesus.
You know the name but not his face.
Come, it's time for you to meet."

*It was good for me to be afflicted so that I might
learn your decrees. The law from your mouth is
more precious to me than thousands of pieces of sil-
ver and gold.* Psalm 119:71–72

And we know that in all things God works for the good of those who love him, who have been called according to his purpose. Romans 8:28

For I know the plans I have for you," declares the LORD, *"plans to prosper you and not to harm you, plans to give you hope and a future. Then you will call on me and come and pray to me, and I will listen to you. You will seek me and find me when you seek me with all your heart.* Jeremiah 29:11–13

Words of Comfort

When I was about nineteen years old and trying to find my way through a long period of low-level depression, God gave me a dream to counter a lie straight from hell. Even though I had always believed in God, I could never feel his presence back then. Since I knew he was a loving God and my heart longed to be close to him, I assumed the problem was with me. Perhaps, as everyone told me, I just wanted too much. This was the dream he sent to combat that lie.

I spotted God across an enormous field. I was beside myself with joy because I wanted *so* much to be near him, to talk with him. At first, he appeared to be waiting for me, but once I began to move toward him, he started walking away. I sped up and finally began to run, but I couldn't seem to reduce the distance between us. Fearful that this precious moment was going to slip away, I called out to him. To my dismay, he kept walking, seemingly unable to hear me.

Abruptly, I sensed I had come to some type of invisible barrier that I somehow knew was impossible to skirt around or scale. I could go no further! I pounded on whatever this was that stood between my God and me. I felt the most excruciating sense of loss standing there, calling for him even as I watched him slowly disappear.

I vividly remember feeling hope drain from my heart because at that moment I knew I would never have an opportunity like this again. Then from behind me came a voice that whispered so tenderly, "*I'm right here.*"

I woke up, knowing immediately that God had spoken to me. He knew how much I wanted him, and he knew that my brokenness perceived a barrier that was merely a product of my imagination. In his mercy, he had orchestrated a dream to tell me, "I'm not out there somewhere, and I'm never unreachable. I'll always be close enough to whisper right in your ear. Daughter, I would *never* walk away from you."

"Am I only a God nearby," declares the Lord, "and not a God far away? Jeremiah 23:23

The Lord is near to all who call upon him, to all who call upon him in truth. Psalm 145:18

When you pass through the waters, I will be with you; and when you pass through the rivers, they will not sweep over you. When you walk through the fire, you will not be burned; the flames will not set you ablaze. When you pass through the waters, I will be with you; and when you pass through the rivers, they shall not overflow you. When you walk through the fire, you shall not be burned; the flames will not scorch you. Isaiah 43:2

The Lord himself goes before you and will be with you; he will never leave you nor forsake you. Do not be afraid; do not be discouraged. It is the Lord who goes before you. He will be with you; he will not leave you or forsake you. Do not fear or be dismayed. Deuteronomy 31:8

Lies of the Enemy

W hat I share with you here was my first *recognizable* experience with the lying voice of our spiritual enemy, Satan. Even in the midst of it, though, God's voice broke through like a brilliant beacon and his sovereign authority prevailed.

I had only been following Jesus for a week or so. Because my conversion experience had been lonely and painful, being able to sense God's presence whenever I reached out was comforting like nothing I had ever experienced before. Feeling known, cherished, and safe in God's hands was heavenly. Needless to say, I was purely ecstatic that afternoon as I set out on a walk with my dog, Spanky.

The sun was hot enough to raise heat waves from the pavement, but oh that breeze! The smell of freshly cut grass filled my senses, as did the sound of birds calling to each other high above me in the trees. Amazingly, even my dog seemed to be content. He trotted along ahead of me instead of yanking me down the street as he usually did.

Partway into our walk, he stopped to burrow his nose in the grass. I took that opportunity to close my eyes and raise my face to the sun. I was caught up in relishing the moment when awareness dawned. It wasn't just the sun I was enjoying. I was basking in something I had not felt in a long time—hope. God was with me, and I was certain that he had good things ahead for me.

It was such a relief to realize that I had relinquished the burden of keeping myself from plummeting into the abyss of hopelessness that had loomed in front of me for what seemed like forever. I had finally put that impossible task into the hands of someone who was actually strong enough to do it. God had control of the universe, and it seemed that, for that moment at least, my only job was to enjoy him. Peace and contentment saturated my entire being.

Then, out of nowhere, came this nasty voice in my head: *This can't possibly last!*

Words cannot convey the impact that statement had on my heart. I was old enough to know how often solutions that appear perfect at first tend to fail after a while. My stomach cramped with horror because at that moment I felt certain I would be going back down into that familiar pit of despair. I was also sure that this time there would be no escape. After all, if God wasn't enough, nothing would be!

I only hung in that hellish state for a few seconds before another voice said with such calm confidence: *That is a lie. Nothing will ever be the same again.* In that instant, God granted me understanding that it had been a demon who had whispered that horrible lie into my head and that it was my Savior who had responded to it. The best part was that I also knew, with absolute certainty, which of those voices spoke the truth. I recognized that I had just had my first lesson in spiritual warfare.

I felt the incredible nearness and protection of my heavenly Father. He used the devil's attempt to frighten me as a teaching tool. He wanted me to learn to distinguish between his voice and Satan's. Experiencing God's authority as he summarily silenced my adversary was thrilling indeed.

…He (Satan) was a murderer from the beginning, not holding to the truth, for there is no truth in

him. When he lies, he speaks his native language, for he is a liar and the father of lies. John 8:44

Be alert and of sober mind. Your enemy the devil prowls around like a roaring lion looking for someone to devour. 1 Peter 5:8

The great dragon was hurled down—that ancient serpent called the devil, or Satan, who leads the whole world astray. He was hurled to the earth, and his angels (demons) with him. Revelation 12:9

The thief (Satan) comes only to steal, kill and destroy. I (Jesus) have come that they may have life, and have it to the full. John 10:10

His Lap

You have undoubtedly heard this all before. I had been married to a good man for about twelve years, I lived in a beautiful home, and I had two healthy children. Even though I had so much to be grateful for, I still felt *incredibly* lonely and unfulfilled.

I wrote the original version of what you are about to read late one night as I sat alone in my family room. It wasn't until I came into a relationship with Jesus some twenty years later that I realized what I'd written that night wasn't just something out of my imagination. It had been a gift directly from God's loving heart to me, his hurting daughter.

He was sitting in a chair before a welcoming fire, waiting for me. I experienced the strangest need to hide even as I longed to run to him. His silent invitation to come closer cut through my confused thoughts and calmed the hammering of my heart. I moved toward the chair directly across from him.

"Is that really where you want to sit?" he asked softly. Even though his question was gentle and inviting, I felt my face redden at having my secret desire exposed. He spoke with incredible compassion, "Dear one, don't you know? I *love* that you want to be close. Wouldn't you rather sit right here with me?" I stared at my feet, too embarrassed to admit just how much I yearned to be close to him.

His patience filled my senses so that, at last, I managed to nod. I felt his deep pleasure as he drew me up onto his lap and wrapped his powerful arms tightly around me. I wished that somehow I could just melt into him. At the same time, I also felt compelled to resist the deep comfort I found in his embrace. Once again, he addressed my thoughts without a word from me.

"Daughter, intimacy is a good thing," with a finger under my chin, he raised my face to look at him, "A blessed thing." The joy that arose at his assurance was exquisite, and for a moment my heart soared. Sadly, before long a familiar hunger began to creep up behind my joy, and with it the painful certainty that my longing would never be completely fulfilled. Sitting warm and protected in his comforting arms made the ache nearly unbearable. His voice cut through my thoughts.

"Why do you think you will never be satisfied?"

The answer fairly burst from me. "Because I want too much!" Shame and self-loathing ripped through me. I wanted desperately to hide my naked soul.

He held me close and whispered, "Allow that little one inside of you speak, beloved. You have denied her a voice for so long. Her emotions won't consume you; I promise."

He raised my chin, once again urging me to look at him. The understanding in his eyes tugged gently at the callus that covered my heart. I drank in the tender acceptance he poured into me even as I fought a desperate need to look away. When the pressure became too intense, I finally relinquished control. With that, years of loneliness and disappointment fouled by shame, guilt, and anger began to pour out in my hot tears. He rocked me gently as he ministered to me through my sobs.

"It hurt me to see your precious little soul being bruised, betrayed, and neglected. I gave you a sweet, open heart and an extra measure of sensitivity. Unfortunately, the world disdains those things as weakness, and how it *delights* in stomping on weakness! Dear heart, your need to give and receive love are certainly not too much! However, starve a heart and label its needs unnatural long enough, and it will finally turn upon itself, pushing away its deepest longing as something undeserved and somehow even disgraceful. You thought your only option was to close yourself off to the very things I created you to desire. My love, your ache for more is *not* a thing to be scorned!"

He let that blessed truth reach my heart before saying more. "But, dearest one, that need can only be satisfied in me." He fell silent and I stared into his magnificent eyes while his truth began to take fragile root. At last, his gentle peace settled firmly upon me. Finally, he smiled and released my gaze. I leaned into him, took a deep breath and rested. I don't know how long we sat that way, but in time, I felt him stir.

"Hear me now, child. I Am! If you would but receive it, I will give you all the love, affirmation, and attention you need. You are my perfect creation, and you are so *incredibly* beautiful. I have so much I want to show you when you are ready. Until that time, I want you to lay down the idea that your childlike need for love and connection is somehow wrong. Little one, growing up spiritually does not mean that you must do life on your own."

I looked up at him, confused by the lies pouring into my head. As if in answer, I felt his arms tighten around me. "Daughter, you may stay right here on my lap forever and ever. Stay while I heal that little girl's heart. And then stay—just because we like it."

Give thanks to the God of heaven. His love endures forever. Psalm 136:26

He will wipe every tear from their eyes. There will be no more death or mourning or crying or pain, for the old order of things has passed away. Revelation 21:4

Don't be deceived, my dear brothers and sisters. Every good and perfect gift is from above, coming down from the Father of the heavenly lights, who does not change like shifting shadows. James 1:16–17

Getting Out of the Boat

May I tell you about a horrible/wonderful time of testing and growth in my life? God used it to show me things about myself, about spiritual warfare and most importantly, about who he is. He also used this experience to convince me that he knows precisely how much stretching I can handle. He knew that on one particular morning, my ability to stand was failing. So, at precisely the right moment, he stepped between my enemy and me and said, "Enough!"

I had been a committed follower of Jesus for three years when an opportunity arose to go on a three-week mission trip to Africa. At that time, I had no idea how deep my fear and trust issues ran. That is because I kept them out of my awareness by living life almost entirely within my comfort zone. I accomplished that by avoiding things that made me too uneasy.

At the same time, I had always been one of those all-in kind of people who doesn't do anything halfway. That part of me wanted to dive in and *do* this thing! I wanted to see God at work, and I wanted him to use me to heal and love his children.

I believe God created me to live large, but every time I thought about committing to the trip, a wrenching fear settled on me. All I knew to do was pray for guidance as to whether I was supposed to go and ask God to remove this ridiculous fear.

One morning, as I was once again wrestling with what to do I heard God say to my spirit, "Step off that cliff. I will catch you, and we will soar together." Wow! How much clearer could he be? I turned in my application the next day. After all, who wouldn't want to soar with Jesus? I was still afraid, but I figured I had almost a year to grow and prepare. At the time, I believed God would surely deal with this fear thing before I had to leave.

At our first team-building meeting, our pastor asked everyone to share his or her hopes for the trip. My heart started racing because this whole thing had suddenly become *way* too real. I confided that, as dramatic as it sounded, I just hoped to survive emotionally. The room grew quiet, and all eyes turned toward me. I could barely control my voice when I explained that I thought this trip was more about God doing something *in* me than about anything he would accomplish through me. My pastor gently acknowledged my apprehension and complimented me on the maturity of that understanding. The team prayed for me, and then we moved on to logistics.

I was dutifully taking notes so that I would not forget anything I needed to do, when my pastor said something that jolted me right back into panic mode. He told everyone that he was going to have a lot on his plate this trip and that he wasn't there to coddle us. He reminded us that we were all leaders in the church and that he expected us to handle ourselves accordingly. While I completely understood his point, I felt solid ground crumbling rapidly beneath my feet. As much as I tried to pay attention to the rest of the meeting, my anxiety and sense of isolation made that nearly impossible.

On the drive home, I tried to steel myself with faith, but there was no ignoring the horror creeping ever closer in the dark. The frightened little girl inside of me was shouting *I know I have to do this. I want to do this, but he just told me that I have to do it alone!* My distress became so overwhelming that I had to stop the car and give myself over to the release of tears.

Some days, I would barely feel the dread that settled on me that night. Other days, it became nearly intolerable, but it never left entirely. I had committed myself, and now I felt trapped.

I awoke the morning after that team meeting with the understanding that God was taking me back to a place where I had experienced a deep wounding with my father when I was six years old. My dad was a lonely, isolated man who lived in the past. While on a rare family vacation, he took my five-year-old brother and me to his favorite place, the place where he lived in his imagination, namely the woods of Pennsylvania.

On our hike, we came to what felt like a ravine to my six-year-old self. Dad found a log he said we could use to cross it and then proceeded to lead the way. With encouragement, my younger brother made it across. At first, my father said encouraging things to me too. "It only looks hard. All you have to do is start walking." It didn't matter. I was too afraid to try, and the impatience I could see on my father's face only fueled my fear. Desperate and embarrassed, I finally got down on my hands and knees. *If I can't walk across, perhaps I can crawl.* His stern "No, get up and walk!" sent a dagger of fear through my little soul. I could *not* do this, and my daddy was getting mad at me. Frustrated, he finally shook his head, took my brother's arm, and began to walk away. I couldn't cross to be with them, and I had no idea how to get back to the car. They were going to leave me there—and it was my own fault!

Obviously, my father came back and he didn't make me cross the log. Nevertheless, I could almost taste his disappointment in me. I loved my daddy, and he had made it plain that I had ruined his time in the woods. I couldn't have articulated it then, but I was thoroughly ashamed of myself. After all, my little brother had no problem crossing that stupid log. That could mean only one thing: there was something wrong with me!

Yes, my current situation felt very much like that one. Once again, I was being asked to face something that felt like death to me—all alone. Telling myself that this time I had God with me and that I was a fully functioning adult didn't really help. God was putting me back into the position where I feared being such a colossal disappointment and burden on people that they would want to abandon me. Intellectually, I knew God had something good for me in this trial, or he would never put me through it.

Unfortunately, that's a lot like trying to console a child who is afraid of getting a shot by assuring them that it is actually a good thing.

Interestingly, over the next few months, I began to sense in myself something the prophet Isaiah said prophetically about Jesus. *Because the Sovereign Lord helps me, I will not be disgraced. Therefore have I set my face like flint, and I know I will not be put to shame.* Isaiah 50:7.

I thanked the Lord for giving me that kind of resolve. Unfortunately, lasting peace didn't accompany it. But at least he gave me the determination that nothing that my flesh nor my enemy would throw at me was going to stop me from doing this thing—period.

One day, I asked my women's group leader why, if the enemy could see as plainly as I could that he wasn't going to stop me from going, didn't he stop trying? Her answer was as simple as it was profound. "Because he loves making you uncomfortable. He *enjoys* seeing you miserable. He wants to distract you, hoping you'll miss out on what God has for you today because you're living in dread of tomorrow." How right she was.

To my dismay, the day finally came. At 10:30 a.m. on Friday, July 30, 2010, I boarded the first of the three flights on my journey to South Africa. We finally landed at 8:30 p.m. on

Saturday, July 31. Several lovely people from the Vineyard church in Durban were there to greet and take us to our host homes for a much-needed rest.

The local pastor's wife had arranged for me to stay in the home of a young mother recently diagnosed with cancer. She later told me that since the woman's husband wasn't a believer, she was hoping that my presence would be a blessing to this sweet woman. As loving as her intentions were, it wasn't wise for me to be isolated from my team. One of the devil's strategies is to divide and conquer and, as a relatively new Christian, I didn't have the maturity to stand up to his harassment alone.

This kind family gave me a room with an incredible view of Moses Mabhida Stadium. I quickly unpacked, got my clothes ready for church the next morning, and went to bed. Unfortunately, sleep eluded me most of the night. It seemed that every time I started to drift off, something would yank me back to consciousness. I tried to pray. I tried to imagine the amazing things God was going to do on this trip. Nevertheless, thoughts of being late, of getting sick, of trying to fit in, and of being a burden to others kept intruding. I averaged about three hours sleep those first few nights, so each day I got progressively more exhausted which, in turn, made me weaker in spirit.

I don't want to give the impression that everything about this trip was negative because that wasn't the case. I met some wonderful people with totally awesome accents! My pastor led three powerful equipping sessions for local pastors during which I had the privilege of praying for several people. God gave me the opportunity to see how incredibly blessed we Americans are. I walked on the beach of the Indian Ocean. I got to enjoy giant intricately molded sand sculptures that the locals had created. We spent a day on "safari" at a local wildlife preserve where a family of rhinos napping on the road held us hostage for a full half hour. There could be no doubt that this was a once-in-a-lifetime opportunity. God was clearly at work in my heart. I think excerpts from my journal tell it best.

Aug 2, 2010 (Day 4): Father, this is the hardest thing I can *ever* remember attempting. I know you are doing a wonderful work in me. I want to submit fully to you, but I don't know how to *be* in this position. This stretching is *so* painful and scary. I have been trying to guard my thoughts, stay in the present, cast my fears on you, and speak truth to counter the lies the enemy is telling me. Lies like *"You don't belong. You are a burden. You don't have anything to offer these people. You're a fake. You're going to get sick. You look like a fool. You won't survive this. Who do you think you are, wanting to soar with Jesus anyway?"*

I know I'm not displeasing you, Father, but please show me how to do this. I want to learn how to be joyful in all circumstances. You have shown me that I idolize control and comfort, and I know that has to change. I can also see that I tend to cling to people rather than to you, and that opens the door for the devil to torment me whenever people aren't giving me whatever I feel I need each moment. Please change me. I don't want anything left standing between us. It feels like your transforming fingers are pressing very hard on me right now. I ask you to help me stay on your potter's wheel. I open myself fully to you (as much as I'm able today). Please free me from these chains of doubt and fear. I long to soar with you!

Aug 4, 2010 (Day 6): Today was our first trip to Mayville (a shanty town with no electricity, water, or sanitation). We assembled at our host church to pack up bags of donated clothes and blankets to distribute. Once we got to the site, we divided into groups. My group went to the houses of two schoolgirls our host church was sponsoring. We had to climb very steep, very narrow steps up the side of a hill to get to the first house. The elderly lady there was raising three orphaned kids without any physical, emotional, or financial help. As we prayed for her, my heart started to ache.

I stepped up onto the raised cement block she was standing on and said to her, "God sees your loneliness." The tears in her eyes tore at my soul. I put my arms around her and whispered words of encouragement. I felt a connection building, but by then it was time to leave. Jesus, you know how hard it was for me to leave her in such loneliness. I knew I couldn't fix her situation, but it felt so wrong to touch her pain like that and then just walk away. You are her savior, not me. Please teach me how to do this!

After we finished passing out clothes and blankets, the team went out for supper. I wanted to join in, but I didn't fit comfortably with any of the groups. There were pastors, couples, and a group of long-time friends who were younger than my children. Of course, it didn't help that I couldn't hear enough of any of the conversations to actively participate. I tried to stay engaged but felt myself losing the battle with self-pity.

Father, the voices in my head have been relentless throughout this trip. *Nobody actually wants to talk to you. They are just being kind when they include you. Have you noticed how quickly they move on to other people? Face it, you are irrelevant.*

Jesus, help me fight these pervasive lies. Tell me the truth about my relationships. Please heal me. Show me how to get from you what I need to feel whole. Teach me to turn to you when I feel lonely and rejected rather than dig another empty well. Please set me free!

Aug 5, 2010 (Day 7): Not every American gets to celebrate a birthday in Africa! In addition to the fact that I am still averaging only about four hours of sleep per night, I woke this morning with diarrhea. I rode waves of fear about getting typhoid from the salad I ate yesterday. Father, protect me. I can't refuse to eat the food people prepare for me. Two of my church's associate pastors prayed for me before we left to do the second pastor's conference, but I still feel off balance. It is cold, cloudy, and windy, and I feel so isolated. I don't want to talk to anyone. I don't want to minister to anyone. All I want right now is to go home and feel normal.

As the team chatted and laughed over breakfast, I went off by myself intending to pray. When I couldn't do much more than groan, and I couldn't discern God's voice at all, I gave up and resigned myself to just getting through the rest of the trip. I curled up on a couch, purposely isolating myself. But because I still wanted to honor God and my teammates, I roused myself when the conference attendees started to arrive.

As usual, we opened the session with worship. The words to the first song, "You Never Let Go," by Matt Redman and Lawrence Gowan described what I was feeling at that moment so perfectly that I collapsed into my chair unable to hold back the tears. I didn't care who saw this "missionary" wailing like a baby in her chair. I can vividly remember the relief that washed over me at hearing God assure me through the song that even though I felt too weak to hold onto him, he would never let go of me.

It is hard to describe the next three or so minutes. Our miraculous God used the words of that song somehow to enable me to recognize that a battle was being fought over me in the spiritual realm. Oddly, I could sense it going on both inside and all around me.

At first, as I sat there crying, I wanted to close myself to this painful work God was doing in me. I wanted *nothing* more than to go home and feel emotionally safe again. One of my teammates came over, laid her hand on my shoulder and prayed for me as the song (and the battle) continued.

Looking back, I can see that territory was being taken back in the spirit world as my friend stood praying over me. In turn, the retaking of that ground shifted something inside of me. I felt my spiritual strength returning. At first, I just felt Jesus encouraging me. To my surprise, I began to feel a tremendous longing for him bubbling up from deep inside of me. Before long my desire to soar with my Savior returned (I hadn't even noticed it leaving).

Next, God let me know that I needed to speak it out, to announce my intention to the powers of darkness. He had stepped between the enemy and me. Not only had he silenced the father of lies, but he had also strengthened my spiritual legs so that I could once again have a hope of standing against him myself. I have never felt as empowered as I did at that moment. Even though it's doubtful that anyone was paying the slightest attention to me, I can't help but smile when I contemplate what people would have thought to see me jump up in the middle of the song and shout, "I *will* stay engaged!"

God spent the next year showing me things about that trip. Even though I was too off-balance to recognize it at the time, it's clear to me now that Satan was winning the battle as I laid on that couch wrapped up in a blanket. I knew all along that deciding to disengage my heart to get through the rest of the trip was not God's best for me. However, I had no idea that the enemy of my soul was after *so* much more than that small victory.

My heart's desire is to follow the Apostle Peter's example and, in faith, get out of my safe little boat. I want to walk on water with Jesus, or as he put it, "Step off that cliff and soar with me." However, I vividly remember thinking that morning *Jesus, if this is soaring, I'd really rather not.* Allowing myself to entertain that kind of thought only led to more shaming and defeatist thoughts. *Who in blazes did I think I was to even imagine that someone as weak as me could walk on water in the first place?* I pictured myself slinking back into the boat and sitting down, willing to shut my mouth forever about wanting God to use me to make a deep and lasting impact in his kingdom.

Weeks after the trip, God showed me why that battle had been so intense. What Satan was actually after that morning was my ability to trust Jesus, in any substantive way, in the future. The powers of darkness knew that with that type of failure to look back on, I might never have been willing to step out of my comfortably safe box again. There was no way God was going to allow that!

Several months after I returned, God showed me still another powerful truth through this experience. Although intellectually I knew I had done my very best to trust him while I was there, I could not shake the feeling that I had failed because my trust had not made me peaceful. One day, Jesus asked me, "Would you be angry at yourself for being afraid the first time you went sky-diving?" I told him I wouldn't because fear would be a reasonable reaction in that situation. He said, "This isn't any different. How can you expect to trust me until I show you that I am trustworthy? Given the height this leap represented for you, I felt honored by the level of trust you chose to put in me."

"Come," he said. Then Peter got down out of the boat, walked on the water and came toward

Jesus. But when he saw the wind, he was afraid and, beginning to sink, cried out, "Lord, save me!" Immediately Jesus reached out his hand and caught him. "You of little faith," he said, "why did you doubt?" Matthew 14:29–31

"I will instruct you and teach you in the way you should go; I will counsel you with my loving eye on you." Psalm 32:8

In the same way, the (Holy) Spirit helps us in our weakness. We do not know what we ought to pray for, but the Spirit himself intercedes for us through wordless groans. Romans 8:26

"For I know the plans I have for you," declares the Lord, "plans to prosper you and not to harm you, plans to give you hope and a future. Jeremiah 29:11

PART 2

Introspection, Grief, and Self-Centeredness

<hr>

What place does looking inward have in the life of a Christian who longs to love well and selflessly? That question has been on my mind for quite some time. On the one hand, I am incredibly aware of how self-centered I am. That is, I tend to see everything in light of how it pertains to me. At the same time, I also know that God created me to be contemplative. Because of the way he wired me, I *naturally* give a lot of thought to what happens to me and around me, as well as how I react to those things.

My confusion stems largely from differing teachings I've heard about this subject. One group maintains that introspection has little place in the life of a Christian. Others claim that in order to know God, we must truly get to know ourselves. While I believe that both statements are at least partly true and that balance is the key, I often struggle to discern the point when natural introspection becomes unhealthy or even sinful.

I decided to explore this subject in more depth because something brought me face-to-face with unresolved pain in my life. Because this sorrow wasn't new, my tears surprised me. But what shocked me more than the fact that it could still cause more than a wistful sigh was the realization that it felt wrong to permit myself to be sad about it this many years later. When the same thing happened the next day with a different situation, I knew God was up to something. Some explanation is in order.

A book I was reading contained a beautifully tender scene between a mother and daughter. As I read, I could feel an uncomfortable mix of longing, jealousy, and anger stirring within me. Moments of intimacy like that are rare between my daughter and me. I think we both want to be close, but intimacy requires trust, and we haven't been emotionally safe with each other for a long time.

I believe God was showing me that, even though I have always been aware of my longing for a satisfying relationship with my daughter, I have done my best to suppress that desire. That seemed a strange thing to do until it occurred to me that in doing that, I was subconsciously protecting myself. It just seemed foolish to continue wanting something I could not have.

I think God also wanted to highlight an error in my thinking. I have always believed that because he had promised me that my daughter would one day be an "awesome Christian," it was wrong for me to have feelings about the way he did it or how long he took to get it done. God showed me that, while it is life-giving for me to keep his promise about her future foremost in my mind, he does not want me to deny how sad I feel to have missed out on nearly thirty years of closeness with her.

The other situation I mentioned came via another scene from that same book. The main character who thought she could never have a child finally gets to cuddle her newborn baby. This scene impacted me on more than one level. The first thing that struck me was how often I have wished I could get a do-over, whereby the person I am today could raise my children instead of the woman I was when they were small. Also, because I am most likely in the last quarter of my life, I can't wait to spoil some grandchildren!

But the deepest level of anguish, the one I have never really allowed to surface, is that I have lost four little ones to death. Naturally, I felt sad at the time, but I believed that my focus needed to be on my family. I wanted to help them through whatever they were experiencing. I grieved the loneliness, confusion, and anger *they* lived with every day. I was also acutely aware of the anguish their pain caused God. After all, he carried the sorrow of every person involved. Somehow, though, I never dealt with how these losses affected me personally. It seemed too self-centered to think about that.

Shortly after reading that book, I felt God encouraging me to take inventory of losses I have experienced over the years. He then asked me to consider why I tend to brush them aside. As I made my list, I soon recognized a familiar and wickedly condemning voice that chimes in whenever I open certain forbidden doors in my heart.

Loss	Condemning Words I Hear
I lost both of my parents early in life.	Stop feeling sorry for yourself! That was more than thirty-five years ago. Are you daring to compare your loss to that of people who never had parents at all? What about the people who lost parents much earlier in life than you?

Something was missing for me on my wedding day. The feeling that came over me as I stood looking in the mirror with two other brides was, "They're the real brides, you are an impostor."	What is *wrong* with you? You had a beautiful wedding. Can't you ever be happy?
I never got an "Oh, sweetheart, that's wonderful!" reaction from my husband about any of my pregnancies.	Poor you. So he didn't gush over your being pregnant—so what? You're always seeking attention.
Babies taken from me.	Oh, poor you! Don't you ever think about anyone besides yourself?
Unfulfilling relationship with my daughter.	Again with the whining about what you want and what you don't have. You should be grateful. At least you *have* a daughter.
My husband is antagonistic toward the things of God. I am a spiritual widow.	Get over yourself and start focusing on what's right about the man God gave you. Perhaps if you were a nicer person…

Do you hear the enemy's voice as he spoke to me? He ridicules me for wanting good things. He tells me I am ungrateful, and he drowns me in the fear of being self-indulgent and self-absorbed. He uses that distressing combination to make me eager to avoid the very pain Jesus wants to heal.

I have learned that one of the devil's most successful tricks is to sneak his lies in with the truth. He knows that recognizing some truth in what he hisses at me will subconsciously make me more willing to accept the rest of what he says. For example, I do need to focus on the significant amount of good in my husband. Nevertheless, doing that doesn't make it any easier to live with someone who disdains God and finds my love for him foolish.

Another of Satan's dirty tricks is to tell me the truth and then encourage me to come to a false conclusion about that truth. Here are some examples from my life of how he does that:

Truth	False Conclusion
I *should* be endlessly grateful for all God has done for and given to me.	It is bad to long for things he hasn't given me.
I am not honoring God when I allow my focus to become stuck on myself and my wants.	For that reason, allowing myself to experience negative emotions when they arise is self-indulgent and sinful.
Our emotions *can* deceive us, and they *can* lead us astray.	Therefore, we must do our best to ignore our feelings.

I honor God when I open my broken heart, as well as my wildest dreams to him as my Father, my healer, and my provider.	But he gets *really* tired of hearing about me!
It pleases God when I trust him enough to hold my dreams and desires with expectant but open hands.	But God helps those who help themselves. (Contrary to popular opinion, this old saying is *not* biblical. In fact, the Bible teaches total dependence on God.).
It is entirely possible to seek godly desires in my own strength or in ways that do not honor him.	Therefore, it is safer all around to avoid wanting things I do not have.

Here's the problem: God created us to live Edenic lives. At creation, he intended all of our relationships to be blessedly full and mutually satisfying. He designed us for perfection on every level. Our desire for that did not magically disappear when God banished us from Eden. The fall put actual perfection out of reach while we live on this earth, but our hearts will *always* long for it.

Without a doubt, we can turn even good things into deadly idols. And, yes, we can go astray by trying to meet our legitimate needs in ungodly ways. The good news is that Jesus is willing to help us with that. But, since God is committed to not violating our free will, we are wise if we cooperate by bringing our stuff out of hiding and willingly exposing it to his blessedly redemptive light.

If any of you lacks wisdom, you should ask God, who gives generously to all without finding fault, and it will be given you. James 1:5

Now this is eternal life: that they know you, the only true God, and Jesus Christ, whom you have sent. John 17:3

Search me, God, and know my heart; test me and know my anxious thoughts. See if there is any offensive way in me, and lead me in the way everlasting. Psalm 139:23–24

Lady in Red

What I write here was initially part of the previous chapter entitled "Introspection, Grief, and Self-Centeredness." When God kept bringing me back to the subject of losses I have experienced in my life, I finally allowed him to take me to a very lonely place, one he wanted to speak into. Because I think this subject is significant and nearly universal to women, I want to explore it in more depth.

God used the song "Lady in Red" by Chris de Burgh to touch a wound I have worked hard to ignore for a long time. I had avoided even listening to it for years because, to be honest, whenever I did, I felt this sense of embarrassment for wanting what it illustrates so beautifully. It felt juvenile, almost idiotic, to allow myself to imagine someone feeling that way about me. "Lady in Red" poked bruised areas in my heart, places that ached to be seen and found to be beautiful both inside and out. Places that long to be, dare I say it—adored.

Because allowing myself to experience that desire always aroused the ugly emotions of self-pity and resentment, I told myself that it was better not to want what I couldn't have. The ridiculing voice of my spiritual enemy was always there to taunt me: *That is such a stupid song! They only wrote it to sell music to overly emotional women. Men only pretend to feel that way.* Unfortunately, because my life experiences reinforced those thoughts, I bought into the deceiver's lie. Even so, a part of me knew what he was saying wasn't completely true. That all-in kind of love does exist. Unfortunately, once I threw off Satan's first lie, he quietly switched to another one. *It does exist—just not for you.*

The idea of "not for you" is something Satan has successfully used against me for years. That statement allowed him to tell me that I couldn't have whatever good thing I wanted without his having to convince me that God was the problem. God showed me that in my mind, if something "wasn't for me" there were only two possibilities. Either God had other plans (which are always better than mine), or something about me was keeping the good thing away. Can you see how cleverly the enemy of my soul arranged it so that I would not question his lie that this wonderful thing I longed for might exist but just wasn't available to me?

When at God's urging I played the song again recently, I immersed myself in a painfully delicious ache for perfect acceptance and love, a love I could almost taste but at the same time seemed to be always just out of reach.

As I was writing this, God brought to mind a story my pastor told our church years ago. He described a scene where a handsome young teacher spotted one of the school's not-so-popular girls leaning against the wall at her prom. He said the teacher noticed her corsage-less arm and, smiling, asked her to dance. The usually shy girl beamed as the teacher took her into his arms and led her onto the dance floor. My pastor went on to tell us that Jesus is like that teacher, ever wanting to hold us close, able to lead us effortlessly around his dance floor. He said that all that is required of us is to relax in Jesus' embrace and allow him to lead.

For more than forty years, I have secretly hoped that one day, I would see my husband's eyes grow wide with appreciation when he sees me. I have wanted him to say, "I have been blind." The truth is that I long to be loved in ways that, today at least, are foreign to my dear husband's nature. To him, the kind of sentiment expressed in "Lady in Red" seems ludicrous. The good news is that Jesus doesn't find my desire for deeply romantic connection objectionable in the least. He *created* me to want it because he wants it too.

As I listen to the song, I become that girl standing on the sidelines, aching to see someone light up when they see me. As one song after another draws to a close, my hope slips slowly into despair. I gaze down at my new shoes, hoping to hide the waves of shame that I fear will soon overtake me. *Hope is stupid. I am stupid! I hate the world, and I wish I could sneak away, bury my head in my pillow, and disappear forever!*

Then I hear someone whisper my name. When I raise my eyes, I see Jesus standing at the edge of the dance floor. He is watching me, his face radiating approval. At that moment it dawns on me that the way this song affects me is no accident. My Jesus wrote it for me! He set to music how he feels about me.

Rather than move toward me, my Savior stands in place, hand extended. I sense that he is waiting for me to respond. He is inviting me to believe that he has no hidden agenda and that he means every word.

Does *knowing* how much God loves me satisfy my craving for intimacy here on earth? I would love to say that I never feel lonely or disconnected anymore, but that wouldn't be true. Nevertheless, the loneliness I sometimes feel today is far different from what I used to experience. Today, God's presence is actually tangible. If I had to describe it, I'd say it's like there are always hands of hope underneath me, holding me up. Moreover, every day, as I rest in those very trustworthy hands, he draws me a little closer so that I can see him more clearly. Yes, he is enough for today. Indeed, he is my most bountiful portion! I encourage you to quiet your heart. Listen to him whispering his love and approval into your heart as well.

What no eye has seen, what no ear has heard, and what no human mind has conceived—the things God has prepared for those who love him. 1 Corinthians 2:9

For our light and momentary troubles are achieving for us an eternal glory that far outweighs them all.

So we fix our eyes not on what is seen, but on what is unseen since what is seen is temporary, but what is unseen is eternal. 2 Corinthians 4:17–18

Let the king (Jesus) be enthralled by your beauty; honor him, for he is your lord. Psalm 45:11

For he chose us in him (Jesus) before the creation of the world to be holy and blameless in his sight. In love he predestined us for adoption through Jesus Christ, in accordance with his pleasure and will. Ephesians 1:4–5

You Have a Problem with Me

Ever since God asked me to create my inventory of losses, he been using it in various ways to heal me and help me grow. This is another of those lessons.

Have you ever had God speak to you through someone else's experience? I was listening to well-known Christian author and speaker, John Eldredge, talk about his long-awaited vacation out in the wild. He said that so many things had been going horribly wrong that he finally asked God to tell him what was up. God's answer to him really struck a chord with me: "There are unaddressed issues in your soul. You have a beef with me. Do you want to deal with it?" As much as I didn't like the idea of having a problem with God, I somehow knew that at that moment God was talking directly to me.

Several months earlier, God had laid the groundwork that would allow me to acknowledge the truth of that statement in my own life. During prayer ministry time at church, I had asked a dear friend to pray for me about why, in spite of my best efforts and prayers, I still harbored some resentment toward my husband about his adamant stance that he most certainly did *not* need Jesus even though he had admitted that his brokenness had affected both our children and me.

At the same time, I was also uncomfortably aware that until I have dealt with my own sinfulness, I have no business focusing on what might be wrong with him. I asked my friend to pray for me because I believe that my husband deserves every bit of my love and respect, and I want to be able to give it to him.

My friend was silent for a long time and when she finally spoke; her words shocked me.

"Father, we say *no fair!* It's not fair that Sharon has to watch other people seeming to enjoy things she longs for, things she has prayed about for years." As surprised as I was to hear those words, they rang true for me. Could this be my problem with God?

I know that if I feel strongly about something, God wants me to talk to him about it.

Even so, I can't tell you how *wrong* it feels to presume to speak to God the way my friend did that morning. Whenever feelings like that arise in me, my immediate thought is always: *so that is your attitude after everything he has done for you? How dare you! You know he is continually working for everyone's benefit, you impatient, self-centered, ungrateful wretch!*

Nevertheless, God had made it clear that I had a problem with him and, as much as I didn't like it, I knew he was right. Therefore, I allowed myself to explore the thoughts and feelings that began to surface.

Father, I know you introduced me to the prayer of St. Francis for a reason. I am sure of that because it resonates in my deepest places. Jesus, it's clear that I long to display those traits because you do. I hunger for them because they are what you want from me. Lord, you gave me the almost desperate desire to become a person who seeks to console rather than to be consoled; who seeks to understand more than to be understood; someone who seeks to love more than to be loved.

Just like that, I knew what my problem with God was. I took a deep breath, leaned into him, and spoke my heart's confusion and pain. "But, Jesus, those are the very things I am starving for myself. How can you possibly expect me to be that selfless with my husband or anyone else when I'm living in emotional and spiritual barrenness myself?"

His compassionate response poured into my heart. *Daughter, it is a process. The key lies in two of the words St. Francis used. He said, "seeks to." Sharon, I know that selflessness is not natural to fallen humankind and believe me; I understand how hard it is to live among spiritually dead people. I encourage you to simply rest in your desire to become more like me and watch me sovereignly make it happen.*

But, when the waiting and seeking become overwhelming, I don't want you to hide your disappointment and frustration from me. Telling me what you honestly feel doesn't disappoint or make me angry. Rather it opens the lines of communication. Until your friend prayed for you, you always rejected those feelings so quickly and thoroughly that I couldn't help you with them without overriding your desire to avoid them. Dear Heart, I gave you this nearly impossible desire to keep you close to me.

Clearly, Jesus doesn't want me to wallow in self-pity, and I have learned that resentment doesn't serve anyone well. I believe he was teaching me the difference between lamenting and grumbling. Scripture contains the Psalms and books like Job and Lamentations to communicate that God *invites* us to lament our hard situations with him. He encourages us to respectfully cry "no fair!" to him so that he can comfort and perhaps correct us. So, what is the difference between lamenting and grumbling?

The Oxford English Dictionary defines the word *lament* as "a passionate expression of grief or sorrow." The laments in Scripture, however, go further than just releasing pent-up emotions. Biblical laments are actually a form of worship because they are also exercises in faith.

To understand this paradigm better, I did some research. I found that most of the psalms of lament have three stages. In the beginning, the person simply cries out to God. They openly voice *whatever* they are feeling. *"I am worn out from my groaning. All night long I flood my bed with weeping and drench my couch with tears."* Psalm 6:6

After this emotional release, the lamenting soul asks for God's help. They ask God to step in and provide for them: *"Do not be far from me, my God; come quickly, God, to help me."* Psalm 71:12

However, throughout a true lament, the person never forgets God's flawless character and his infinite faithfulness. Because they seek to remind themselves of who he is and what he has done, their lament ends with a confession of trust, praise, and worship. A successful lament draws us closer to God. *"I will praise you, Lord my God, with all my heart; I will glorify your name forever."* Psalm 86:12

Faithful complaining does not accuse God of wrongdoing. Rather, it is an honest, groaning expression of what it's like to experience the trouble, anguish, and grief of living in this fallen world. *I cry aloud to the Lord; I lift up my voice to the Lord for mercy. I pour out before him my complaint; before him I tell my trouble.* Psalm 142:1–2

On the other hand, if we never move past the first part of a lament and spend all of our time telling God how hurt or angry feel, we are just grumbling. Grumbling directly or indirectly declares that God is not sufficiently good, faithful, loving, wise, powerful, or competent. Otherwise, he would treat us better or run the universe more effectively. Faithless complaining is actually sinful.

Grumbling is not only offensive to God, it is self-defeating and gives the devil a foothold to work in our lives. We must confess this distasteful attitude to the Lord, and then in his forgiveness we can release those feelings to him.

This chapter used to end there until two friends separately suggested that it didn't feel complete to them. They each challenged me to do a little digging into what else God might be showing me.

As I said, my friend's prophetic cry of "no fair" on my behalf struck a chord with me. Nevertheless, because I never *feel* anger toward God, I had assumed he was using the term "problem" loosely. To me, actual anger toward God is not only inappropriate but downright abhorrent. He is God, and he knows best—period! I genuinely believe that he will use whatever he allows in my life for the ultimate good. So, if I believe that, why is he telling me I have a problem with him?

When I look a little deeper into what I think I heard God say to me earlier in this chapter, I can see that because I don't *want* to be angry with him, I suppress those feelings. However, everyone knows that denied emotions don't just magically disappear. They always work their way to the surface, sometimes in very ugly ways. Was God giving me a partial answer as to why, in spite of how I want to behave, I find it nearly impossible to treat the unbelievers in my life in the ways St. Francis laid out in his prayer? Could it be that in my desire to avoid crying "no fair!"

to God, I inappropriately aim the frustration and disappointment I feel at the very people I long to bless?

In his wisdom and kindness, I think God wanted to make me aware of the seeds of a grumbling spirit that my misguided unwillingness to cry "no fair" to God had planted in my heart.

I know this lesson is far from complete because, even though I wholeheartedly agree with what God has shown me about this so far, it still feels wrong to take exception with *anything* he does. However, because I trust that this is all a part of my ongoing sanctification, I say— *"Search me, God, and know my heart; test me and know my anxious thoughts. See if there is any offensive way in me, and lead me in the way everlasting.* Psalm 139:23–24.

As I gave myself the freedom to voice my "problem" with God, I realized that it makes perfect sense for him to give me the desire to offer others the very things I am hungry for myself. After all, who understands someone's need for deep connection better than someone who lives without it? I've heard it said that the most effective ministries often arise out of the places of our wounding. That's because God never wastes our pain.

Now the people complained about their hardships in the hearing of the Lord, and when he heard them his anger was aroused. Then fire from the Lord burned among them and consumed some of the outskirts of the camp. Numbers 11:1

Do everything without grumbling or arguing, so that you may become blameless and pure, "children of God without fault in a warped and crooked generation." Then you will shine among them like stars in the sky. Philippians 2:14–15

Do not be anxious about anything, but in every situation, by prayer and petition, with thanksgiving, present your requests to God. Philippians 4:6

That Very Same Grace

Even though volumes of material have been written about the subject, there was something about two lines from the hymn "Amazing Grace" that kept snagging my attention until I knew I had to delve into the incredible irony expressed through them.

> 'Twas grace that taught my heart to fear
> And grace my fear relieved

The King James Bible Dictionary defines grace as God's spontaneous gift to people, generous, free, and totally undeserved. It takes the forms of forgiveness, love, divine favor, and a share in the divine life of God.

I have always loved "Amazing Grace," but listening to it after I accepted Jesus was like hearing it for the first time. After all, who can recognize how blind they really are until God lifts the veil and his marvelous light comes streaming in?

The way John Newton constructed these two lines caused me to think about the miracle of God's grace in a way I never had before. Let's examine them separately.

"It was grace that taught my heart to fear."

In this context, the word fear has a multi-layered meaning. On the one hand, the wise person fears the righteous judgment God has promised all throughout the Bible.

Then I saw a great white throne and him who was seated on it. The earth and the heavens fled from his presence, and there was no place for them. I saw the dead, great and small, standing before the throne, and books were opened. Another book was opened, which is the book of life. The dead were judged according to what they had done as recorded in the books. The sea gave up the dead that were in it, and death and Hades gave up the dead that were in them. Each person was judged according to what they had done. Then death and Hades were thrown into the lake of fire. The lake of fire is the second death. Anyone whose name was not found written in the Lamb's book of life was thrown into the lake of fire. Revelation 20:11–15

The fear of God also conveys a sense of deep respect, awe, and a willingness to submit to his supreme authority. Fearing God in that sense means that you seek to remain within the boundaries of his will because doing that gives direction to your life. Because the wise love the Lord, they fear any type of separation from him. Our God knows that until we recognize who he is as well as our state without him, we aren't likely to fear him in either sense of the word.

The fear of the Lord is the beginning of knowledge, but fools despise wisdom and instruction. Proverbs 1:7.

Teach me your way, Lord, that I may rely on your faithfulness; give me an undivided heart, that I may fear your name. Psalm 86:11

The word wretch (used earlier in the song) also carries two meanings, which together describe our fallen condition quite well.

- A deplorably unfortunate or unhappy person.
- A person of despicable or base character.

As I said in an earlier chapter, one of the things God used in my journey toward salvation was a fictional work containing an account of the lives of people who, because they had not accepted Jesus as their savior, were not taken to heaven when Christ returned for his followers.

In addition to teaching me that being good won't get you to heaven, these books did a great job convincing me that I did *not* want to be one of those still on earth under Satan's rule. For the first time in my life, I experienced spiritual fear. Although many scholars do not agree with this version of the end times, God used these books to help me discover that I wanted absolutely no part of eternity without him.

"And grace, my fear relieved."

However, God, being who he is, would not have been satisfied if I had sought him only out of terror. He wasn't interested in simply getting me to buy "fire insurance." He wanted me to turn to Jesus out of respect and love. So, as he does for each of his children, God planned and systematically put into place a complex layering of people and circumstances that brought me to saving faith.

Now we come to the sweet irony that so captured my heart and inspired this writing. It is by God's magnificent grace that we first come to recognize who we really are without Jesus. *"Woe to me!" I (Isaiah) cried. "I am ruined! For I am a man of unclean lips, and I live among a people of unclean lips, and my eyes have seen the King, the LORD Almighty."* Isaiah 6:5

But, my friends, it is that *very same* grace that allows us to first recognize and then accept Jesus's atoning sacrifice for our sins, thereby making us right with God—forever!

With our permission, God reaches deep into our rebellious, lonely souls and touches the spot of our most profound need. If we accept his gift of salvation and make him Lord of our life, he awakens our dead spirit and gives us eternal life. God's grace is more amazing than we will *ever* know—this side of heaven.

He has saved us and called us to a holy life—not because of anything we have done but because of his own purpose and grace. This grace was given us in Christ Jesus before the beginning of time. 2 Timothy 1:9

In him (Jesus) we have redemption through his blood, the forgiveness of sins, in accordance with the riches of God's grace that he lavished on us. Ephesians 1:7–8

And you also were included in Christ when you heard the message of truth, the gospel of your salvation. When you believed, you were marked in him with a seal, the promised Holy Spirit, who is a deposit guaranteeing our inheritance until the redemption of those who are God's possession—to the praise of his glory. Ephesians 1:13–14

PART 3

A Better View of Jesus

In my brokenness, I used to think that the Bible sometimes makes Jesus sound rather clinical. For example, Luke 9:46–47 sounds to me like he is using a child solely as a teaching tool. *An argument started among the disciples as to which of them would be the greatest. Jesus, knowing their thoughts, took a little child and had him stand beside him.*

This perception troubled me because it didn't fit with what I knew about my Savior. Nevertheless, what I know to be true does not always line up with how things feel to me. I was contemplating this verse one day when a very different image began playing itself out across the screen of my mind.

I see Jesus sitting in a dusty clearing surrounded by children. A young boy is climbing on his back, and another contented child is nestled half asleep in the crook of his arm. Two boys jostle for position on his outstretched feet. Hearing his mother's call, the toddler in his arms squirms free and runs off. With both hands now free, Jesus reaches up and pulls the boy who is clinging to his back up and over his shoulder. Standing, he holds the squealing youngster upside down until at last, grinning himself, he rights the boy and sets him on his feet.

Feeling a familiar tug on his arm, Jesus flexes his bicep. Delighted, the boy dangles from Jesus's arm while he walks over to a little girl standing near the well. After gently extracting his arm, Jesus squeezes the boy's shoulder before sending him off to rejoin his friends.

Jesus crouches down beside the little girl, who looks to be about three years old. She studies his face for a moment before she whispers, "Can I sit on your lap now?" Eyes filled with tenderness, Jesus picks her up and walks back toward his disciples, where he settles onto a boulder in the shade. Grasping Jesus's index finger, the little girl pulls his arm snugly around her. Once she wriggles into a comfortable position and settles her head against his chest, Jesus begins to teach those gathered around him.

The crowd grumbles in irritation a few seconds later when the little girl's loud giggle interrupts his story. Smiling conspiratorially, Jesus looks down at her and says very softly, "Does my talking tickle your ear?" At her shy nod, he presses her head to his chest and hums. She sits upright, hand to her ear, looking at him in amazement. Grinning, he winks at her and then laughs aloud at her attempt to wink back. When the ever-impetuous Peter clears his throat, Jesus closes his eyes, understanding yet again how little his apostles understand about what is truly important.

Ignoring Peter's impatience, Jesus gazes down at the child in his arms. Her enormous black eyes never leave his as he brings her chubby hand to his lips and kisses it. Seeing her pleasure, he kisses it repeatedly until she giggles. With a contented sigh, Jesus brushes the curls from her face, then cups her head and holds it close to his chest. Once her thumb finds its way to her mouth, he resumes his teaching.

People were bringing little children to Jesus for him to place his hands on them, but the disciples rebuked them. When Jesus saw this, he was indignant. He said to them, "Let the little children come to me, and do not hinder them, for the kingdom of God belongs to such as these. Truly I tell you, anyone who will not receive the kingdom of God like a little child will never enter it." And he took the children in his arms, placed his hands on them and blessed them. Mark 10:13–16

If anyone causes one of these little ones—those who believe in me—to stumble, it would be better for them to have a large millstone hung around their neck and to be drowned in the depths of the sea. Woe to the world because of the things that cause people to stumble! Such things must come, but woe to the person through whom they come! Matthew 18:6–7

Their Radiant Debut

Every time I listen to Rebecca St. James' version of "In a Moment" by Michael Neale and Joel Smallbone I find myself drawn into the lovely picture it paints about people shedding their broken earthly bodies and dancing blissfully before our Savior in heaven. What follows is my attempt to capture the delight and beauty of that scene.

I see others gathering in anticipation even as I feel the pull myself. All faces turning, gazing for an instant, and then almost as one moving toward that beautiful light. We find our places without hurry or struggle for everyone possesses a somehow perfect vantage point. We are millions upon millions standing there expectantly.

As I watch, an enormous stage appears before us, and on its single chair sits our Savior. Then we know. We are to be witnesses to the formal shedding of earthly brokenness and the debut of new heavenly bodies, bodies as glorious and perfect as our King's.

In turn, Jesus calls each one by name to come forward and mount the steps onto the stage. As they do, every watching saint gains a complete understanding of the particular challenges this person faced on earth. For just a moment, these issues return so that we, as a body, can share the pain and frustration of their limitations before Jesus stretches out his hand and casts them away forever.

The first to come is a woman. Like those who follow, she takes the stage in spirit form. We watch her earthly body take shape. It is so old and bent that she walks facing the ground. Her twisted fingers clutch her walker as she struggles to look up and see Jesus. He gets to his feet and comes to her, resting his hand on her back for a moment before swiping it downward and off. With that movement, we see the years peel away. Her back straightens as if Jesus had cast off a stone. I hear a cheer building as we collectively feel the pain leave her body. She looks down at her now unblemished hands and closes her eyes, a joyful smile lighting her lovely face.

Jesus holds her hands in his, each enjoying this moment of serene intimacy. Her clear green eyes fill with tears of love and gratitude when she opens them to see Jesus beaming at her. She reaches up, kisses his cheek, and then quietly takes her place behind his throne.

The second soul is a man who had contracted severe polio as a child. We briefly experience his twenty-odd years on a respirator. Each of us keenly feels his inability even to breathe on his own. Restoration, in his case, comes as Jesus hands him a baseball. Everyone delights in watching him live out the normal childhood he had never had. As he plays, I see him periodically glancing over at Jesus basking in his unhurried approval.

At the Lord's nod, the boy leaps off the stage, landing as neatly as any Olympic gymnast might. Everyone present celebrates his new sturdy body. At last, blissfully spent, he comes to kneel at Jesus's feet. The saints join him, first in praise and then in reverent silence. In time, when he feels ready, the boy stands and takes his place at the back of the stage beside the first soul.

At first, everyone casts their eyes downward as the next spirit takes on her earthly body because to do otherwise seems too invasive, too uncomfortable. We hesitate to look upon this infant born so severely deformed that she lived for only a few hours. Jesus kneels beside her. We stand in awe, watching each abbreviated limb take shape as he gently caresses it. We witness the straightening of her spine as he traces a line tenderly down her back. Praise erupts when he cups her tiny head, and her enormous brown eyes begin to sparkle with life. When his work is complete, he carries this beloved child back to his chair and sits down with her still cradled in his arms. For unmeasured time, they gaze into each other's eyes. In unison, we sense that she is recognizing love for the first time. Our hearts soar to see her finally reach out and grasp his finger in her little hand.

The body of the next in line is whole and healthy, but we instantly feel the affliction in his mind. He stands, eyes darting about, visibly confused. Fear, anger, and profound distrust contort his handsome face. Jesus calls to him with a gentleness and authority that pierce his paranoia so that he is finally able to cross the stage.

Jesus shows the man the contents of a pitcher and then pours it over his head. I see the word "clarity" ripple in the sparkling liquid as it cascades down his face. As one, the witnesses gasp to see the murky sludge of mental illness pooling at his feet. The man purposefully steps out of the puddle of darkness, smiles up at Jesus, and begins to sing praise. Both his song and his countenance now reflect the peace and calm of a lucid mind.

Although I share in the delight of every renewed body, I am especially excited to see a friend from my church step onto the stage. She had lived courageously with multiple sclerosis for decades. Upon mounting the stairs, her eyes find mine in the crowd. We share a knowing smile, having talked about this day many times. When she approaches Jesus, she bends to kiss his hand and then presses it to her cheek. There is no sense of urgency to move on. Every saint is content to bask with her in her special moment. When she finally looks up, Jesus lays his hand on the top of her head, closes his fingers as if he has captured something, and flings it to the ground. Their eyes meet and hold for a moment before Jesus nods and returns to his seat, a secret smile lighting his face.

My friend, whose atrophied muscles hadn't served her for close to fifty years, rises up on her toes and pirouettes gracefully across the stage. My heart soars to see her new body move with such ease and poise. Jesus stands and begins to applaud for her. At once, the heavens burst into worship and praise at the King's extraordinary gesture of humility.

"Hallelujah! Hallelujah to him who is perfect. Holy are you, God. Holy, unchanging and worthy to be praised! Hosanna in the highest!"

Even lost in worship, I sense Jesus' quiet invitation. It's my turn! At once, I find myself on the stage, watching my body take shape. Once again, I feel the familiar twinges caused by my twisted spine, the sharp, grinding pain of arthritic hips, and the ache from an old shoulder injury. I look up self-consciously to see the multitude experiencing the heavy humiliation of my obesity.

Jesus approaches me shaking his head. My spirit hears his authoritative command, "None of that here!" My shame lifts. I can actually see it leave my body like an odious black vapor. I look up in utter amazement to see my Savior's acknowledging smile.

For just a moment, I wonder whether the others also felt him reaching down deep into their hidden places, fixing things the rest of us couldn't even see. He nods in answer to that unspoken question and places one hand on my back and the other on my right hip. His healing feels like satin coursing through my body, filling every cell with his blessed wholeness.

Tears of joy and longing fill my eyes when Jesus invites me to warm myself, leisurely, in his presence. As he places his hands on either side of my face, I sense him bidding me to look up at him. I recall his promise from Revelation 21 as

his thumbs pass gently over my cheeks absorbing
my tears forever

*He will wipe every tear from their eyes. There will
be no more death or mourning or crying or pain,
for the old order of things has passed away. He who
was seated on the throne said, "I am making everything new!" Then he said, "Write this down, for
these words are trustworthy and true."* Revelation
21:4–5

*But our citizenship is in heaven. And we eagerly
await a Savior from there, the Lord Jesus Christ,
who, by the power that enables him to bring everything under his control, will transform our lowly
bodies so that they will be like his glorious body.*
Philippians 3:20–21

Worship

We aren't aware of the presence of angels in our daily lives because, for the most part, they move among us silently. I believe that our gracious Father granted me a brief glance beyond the veil one Sunday. I don't know whether I saw this vision because our worship that morning was especially powerful, or if he just wanted to bless me. Either way, I will never forget what my spirit saw that day.

I stood there, hands raised, longing to draw nearer to my Savior. Even though my eyes were closed, I began to see angels gathering on beams high above my church's altar (the building has only one story and no exposed beams). I heard them calling to each other, "They worship! They worship!"

Then these heavenly beings took to the air. Some whooshed about the sanctuary excitedly while others simply spread their enormous wings and glided majestically back and forth. Their graceful winged dance seemed to be a natural expression of their adulation as if to do otherwise would be foreign to their nature and was therefore impossible.

Their voices joined ours. My spirit heard many individual songs. Each was subtly different from ours, and yet all were in glorious harmony. I sensed that their participation added something to our worship. At the same time, I had the impression that their adoration had nothing at all to do with us. It had a depth to it that birthed a glorious ache in my heart.

Here and there, I could see angels alight near someone. Invariably, that person would bow their head as the angel's hand came to rest on them. Some would begin to tremble, others to weep, but it was apparent that all felt heaven's touch.

I believe that worship is so central in heaven that angels naturally gather wherever it occurs in our world. To me, that raises the question: if angels, who see him clearly, feel the need to worship, how vital must it be for us? I came away from this vision gifted with a stronger sense of the gift God gave us in worship.

1 Corinthians 13:12 says that while we live on this earth, we see the spiritual world imperfectly, like fuzzy reflections in a mirror, but once Jesus returns we will see everything with perfect clarity. Because even the tiny glimpse I can see today fills me with incredible hope and joy, I cannot *wait* to see what awaits us in heaven!

All the angels were standing around the throne and around the elders and the four living creatures. They fell down on their faces before the throne and worshiped God, saying, "Praise and glory, wisdom and thanks, honor and power and strength be to our God for ever and ever. Amen! Revelation 7:11–12

The twenty-four elders fall down before him who sits on the throne and worship him who lives for ever and ever. They lay their crowns before the throne and say: "You are worthy, our Lord and God, to receive glory and honor and power, for you created all things, and by your will they were created and have their being." Revelation 4:10–11

Then I looked and heard the voice of many angels, numbering thousands upon thousands, and ten thousand times ten thousand. They encircled the throne, the living creatures and the elders. In a loud voice they were saying: "Worthy is the Lamb, who was slain, to receive power and wealth and wisdom and strength and honor and glory and praise!" Then I heard every creature in heaven and on earth and under the earth and on the sea, and all that is in them, saying: "To him who sits on the throne and to the Lamb be praise and honor and glory and power, for ever and ever!" The four living creatures said, "Amen," and the elders fell down and worshiped. Revelation 5:11–14.

Not This One

A child is born, and he sins. As that child grows up, he learns about God's laws, but still, he sins. When the man hears about God's Son, he accepts Jesus Christ as his savior. As promised in his Word, the Lord gives the man his Holy Spirit as a seal unto salvation. The man finds employment, marries, and dutifully sends his children to church. However, because he isn't personally interested in a relationship with Jesus and he never develops an accurate understanding of salvation, he comes to the end of his life unsure of his eternal fate.

He slowly becomes aware of the whir and click of instruments all around him. At first, the familiar sound of his wife's voice is reassuring, but then Amber's anguished words begin to penetrate his fog.

"I can't stand his being in this state any longer. Go ahead, remove the life support." The catch in her voice is unsettling. "I don't want to see him kept alive artificially when there's no hope of a full recovery."

The beeping of one of the machines behind him speeds up even as he feels his heart begin to race at the terrifying significance of her words.

Sensing that her patient may be reacting to their conversation, the nurse raises her voice for his benefit, "Victor, everything is okay. I have your pain medication right here." While swabbing his arm with alcohol, the nurse indicates to Amber that they should continue their conversation in the hall.

Okay? Everything is most definitely not okay! You're talking about killing me! I'm not ready to die! Before his fear can spin further out of control, Victor feels the prick of a needle and, within seconds, his anxiety begins to melt away.

Seeing tears in Amber's eyes, the nurse sets down the medication bottle, puts her arms around the frightened woman and whispers, "I know how unthinkable all of this is for you, but I assure you that he isn't in any pain." She falls silent for a moment before she continues, "Since you signed the papers yesterday, we can get started whenever you're ready, and we can go as slowly, or as quickly as you like. Do you want me to call anyone to be with you?"

"Will you stay with me?"

"I'll be here the entire time."

Amber's reply is barely audible "Okay, go ahead."

In an instant, Victor finds himself a hundred feet in the air. Looking down, he sees two lands. One appears inviting: soft, lush, and so very cool and green. The other looks barren and harsh, all jagged edges and sharp points. Between these, he sees an enormous, unsearchable chasm.

Amber holds her husband's hand as the nurse begins preparations to wean him from the machines that have sustained him physically for weeks. She moves slowly, giving Victor's body an opportunity to resume functioning on its own. More importantly, she thinks, a calm, measured pace allows time for God to do the miraculous, or time for family members to prepare their hearts if he chooses to take their loved one home instead. When all is ready, she turns toward Amber, praying quietly as she waits. At last, Victor's weary wife closes her eyes, takes a deep breath, and nods.

"Thy will be done." The nurse whispers and then presses a button twice, thereby decreasing Victor's breathing assistance by half.

"Look quickly. See that of which you will never partake," comes a nasty voice from behind Victor. "For *you* are going elsewhere." With alarming speed, Victor feels his body careening down toward that horrid, forbidding land of desolation and death. The waves of heat shimmering up from it singe his exposed flesh. He swallows back the bile rising in his throat caused by the putrid stench creeping stealthily into his nose and mouth.

Dread constricts Victor's lungs. "Is this... hell?" A vile chuckle from behind him raises the hair on his arms.

"Not even close! It's more like a place of waiting."

Victor closes his eyes an instant before he lands. Even though he had already resigned himself to broken bones, the sharp snap of his legs is beyond horrifying. It takes several seconds for his mind to register the searing pain that increases exponentially with each passing second.

The beast wastes no time. "Get up and walk with me. I have much to show you."

Looking up to protest, Victor sees his attendant for the first time. Its leathery skin is a sickly shade of brownish gray, reminding him of decaying meat. Its spidery arms reach well below what might have been its knees. Victor gags as the thing draws near, thinking that the unwholesome smell permeating this entire place didn't even approach the loathsome odor wafting from its grotesque body.

"Are you the devil?"

The thing roars with laughter. "Do you actually think the master would take time for you?" Suddenly annoyed, it grabs Victor's arm yanking him to his feet. "Shut up and follow me!"

To Victor's amazement, he doesn't immediately crumple to the ground even given his broken legs. The thing acknowledges his plight with a loud cackle.

"That's the master's incredible design. You have all of the pain, and yet you can still walk, thereby causing more pain!" The thing digs its talons into Victor's shoulder and propels him forward. "Look carefully. I want you to see everything."

The nerves in Victor's legs fire frantic pain messages to his brain, but before long, those from his feet outstrip everything else. He instinctively lifts his leg and gasps to see the flesh peel away from the sole of his foot.

Almost immediately, Victor's body begins to react to the change the nurse made. Amber pales at the sudden change in her husband's heart rate.

"Is he suffering?" she whimpers.

The nurse shakes her head reassuringly, "No, honey. His heart is working harder to get oxygen to his organs, but he's not aware." Touching the heart monitor, she continues, "Why don't we turn this down, so it's less of a distraction?" Though her tone is suggestive, she presses the button to silence the machine without waiting for a response.

Fearsome images form in the darkness engulfing Victor. Some remain hazy while others zoom toward and then past him with such alarming speed that Victor, growing dizzy, closes his eyes. When that fails to conceal the ghastly visions, he covers them with his hands.

"Open your eyes. Open them, or I will do it *for* you!" The thing bellows, clawing Victor's hands away from his face. "Behold what you called your Christian life."

Faces of people he had judged, hurt, ridiculed, and ignored parade before Victor's eyes, so many more than he could process. Shame reddens his cheeks to see images of himself lusting openly after women other than his wife.

Dollar signs dance before his eyes and he immediately knows what they mean. He sees himself hiding income from his family to use for his own selfish pursuits. He cringes, recognizing how he had convinced himself years ago that whatever he thought he could afford to give to the church and the needy was all that God wanted from him.

His thoughts suddenly shift so that he sees himself through the eyes of his young son, extolling good deeds and acts of charity, but puffed up with pride at the doing.

"That kind of behavior deserves much worse than mere hell." The creature growls contemptuously. Victor finds himself agreeing as snatches of scripture race through his mind:

Jesus replied: "Love the Lord your God with all of your heart and with all of your soul and with all of your mind. This is the first and greatest commandment. And the second is like it: 'Love your neighbor as yourself.' Matthew 22:37–39

If I speak in the tongues of men or of angels, but do not have love, I am only a resounding gong or a clanging cymbal. If I have the gift of prophecy and can fathom all mysteries and all knowledge, and if I have a faith that can move mountains, but do not have love, I am nothing. If I give all I possess to the poor and give over my body to hardship that I may boast, but do not have love, I gain nothing. 1 Corinthians 13:1–3

Victor's heart grows unbearably heavy. It pains him to see how many opportunities to love others he routinely shuns because he is too busy and self-involved to bother. He can almost taste Jesus's anger and disapproval!

Just then, he senses a change around him even as he hears the gathering wind. With a shriek, the abomination at his side recoils, anxious to avoid it.

"Liar!" the wind declares. "He is covered by the blood of the Lamb." The creature begins to writhe at the mention of Jesus's blood but somehow maintains its grip on its prey. "Victor is a redeemed and beloved son of the Most High God. Behold the seal I placed on him as a youth. No, this one is *mine!*"

"He is a sinful Son of Adam." The demon screeches in desperation. "He knows what he deserves!"

"As far as the east is from the west, so far has the Lord removed Victor's transgressions from him. Be gone, vile son of perdition!" An unholy howling fills the pit, and the thing releases its hold.

Seeing her husband's body slowly relax, Amber begins to sob, more from relief that his poor body no longer had to fight for every breath than out of grief.

"Look at his face, sweetheart."

"He looks so peaceful!" Amber marvels, touching her husband's cheek.

"He is." The nurse answers with quiet assurance.

"How do you know?"

"Because I know who he's with."

My sheep listen to my voice; I know them, and they follow me. I give them eternal life, and they will never perish; and no one will snatch them out of my hand. John 10:27–28

For sin shall no longer be your master, because you are not under the law, but under grace. Romans 6:14

For it is by grace you have been saved, through faith—and this is not from yourselves, it is the gift of God—not by works so that no one can boast. Ephesians 2:8–9

For God so loved the world that he gave his one and only Son, that whoever believes in him shall not perish but have eternal life. John 3:16

Jesus answered, "I am the way, the truth and the life. No one comes to the Father except through me." John 14:6

The Field

I happily give my brother credit for this snapshot. While we were talking one day, he mentioned that he had an idea for a story. He outlined a scenario where Jesus arranges for a nominal Christian to encounter him through creation. It was such a blessing to work with him in bringing his idea to life.

My day had been long and filled with the small, seemingly urgent, errands that consumed my thoughts and sapped my energy. Finally finished, I gave myself permission to relax for a while. I flopped down in the sweet-smelling grass beneath our willow tree and laid back, arms behind my head. Seeing great snowy clouds slide across the sky, I felt oddly cheated that I hadn't noticed earlier what a perfect day it was.

I was contemplating the odd mix of joy and melancholy such beauty always seemed to stir in me when my cell phone chirped. It was my wife texting an update about the elderly neighbor whom she was visiting in the hospital.

The Doctor says it could be any time. I will call you later. Please pray.

I rolled my eyes because all I could remember about Mrs. Weller was her perpetual crankiness. Somewhat irritated at my wife's penchant for what she called serving others. I quickly put the old woman out of my mind and closed my eyes.

I was drifting toward sleep when I became aware of the music. It had a decidedly otherworldly quality to it, like nothing I had ever heard before. It was almost as if creation itself was singing. Oddly, when I opened my eyes, the heavenly chorus resolved itself into the twitter of birds, the scratching of insects and a gentle wind rustling the leaves and grass—that and one man singing. What a glorious sound!

Curious, I lifted my head, eager to find that voice. I discovered that its owner had a full beard and dark, wavy hair that rested heavily on his shoulders. It was strange to see such a masculine looking man gathering flowers. Still, there was something so intriguing about this stranger that I got up and approached him. He had been on his knees but stood and extended his hand as I drew near, smiling as if he knew me. I told him that I lived next door and heard myself asking him if he would like some iced tea. Looking genuinely pleased, he said he'd love some, but would I mind if he finished what he was doing first?

Looking around, I felt a little disoriented because I couldn't imagine how I could have lived next door to this field for years without realizing how huge and truly stunning it was. *And why had I never seen this neighbor before?*

"Have a look around," he said, "The garden is magnificent this time of day."

I felt something brush my leg. When I looked down, I realized that I was somehow knee deep in a patch of enormous red flowers. Movement to my left proved to be a cluster of bushes heavily laden with lemon-yellow blossoms.

To my surprise, my companion had picked nearly every flower behind us except for those on perhaps a dozen little plants. I wondered, briefly, why he would leave them but found myself distracted by a myriad of scents drifting about on the shifting breeze. On impulse, I bent to smell the ice-blue flowers on the stragglers he had left behind. Finding that they had almost no smell at all, I assumed that to be the reason he'd chosen not to pick them.

Seeing that he was still gathering flowers even though his large brown hands were already overflowing, I asked him how much longer he was going to work. He smiled.

"My father *loves* these flowers. He told me to be sure to gather them all." Still amazed by the splendor all around us, I asked him how he grew a garden as full and lush as this in this climate. Looking around he nodded, "It takes a lot of love and patience to produce a strong, healthy flower. They each have their own unique needs." He cocked his head as if something had just occurred to him, "And those needs change with every season." Seeing my confusion, he explained, "You see, these are prayer flowers."

"Prayer flowers?" I repeated. Intrigued, I surveyed the field again, noting that some of the flowers were scrawny, almost weedy looking, while others were tall, graceful, and quite exquisite. My curiosity mushroomed. "Why are some areas covered with just one type of flower?"

"That happens when many people pray simultaneously about the same person or need. Look closer. There are always subtle differences." That thought seemed to please him.

I watched my friend gently stroke each petal of the delicate pink flowers he was currently tending, noting that he didn't pick any of them. He glanced up to see the question in my eyes. "These are the prayers of brand new believers. They are still quite fragile, so I handle them with special care. Look at their radiance!"

He spotted a small group of slightly withered flowers nearby and gathered them up quickly, saying, "My father is blessed when those who are struggling with their faith still choose to pray." I was surprised to see that many of the plants had thorny stems. When my friend noticed what I was looking at, his expression darkened. "Those are from people who are slowly moving away from my father because they refuse to accept his will. Right now, they are still praying because they are hoping for a different answer. Sadly, their hearts are slowly hardening. I will give each of them individual attention later. Some will eventually come to see my father's heart for them." He was quiet for a moment and then sighed, "The ones who don't will slowly wither away like those." He inclined his head toward the flowers he had left on the bushy plants I'd wondered about earlier. "I'll continue tending them all, but sadly some will die away."

I saw his lips move subtly even as he turned my attention to a type of plant I'd never seen before. For such a small plant, it was weighed down with blossoms. Sunny yellow daisies and magenta-colored mums grew on the same stalk with an unusual orange flower tipped in neon green. They reminded me of a child's drawing. He nodded as if reading my thoughts.

"The little ones always produce the brightest prayer flowers, so big and full of faith. They send up the sweetest fragrance!" he said, eyes shining with pride. "My father loves them so." I watched the smile slip from his face. "But their numbers have been decreasing of late because so many children aren't getting the kind of attention they need to grow spiritually strong."

He turned abruptly, apparently hearing something behind us. I looked to see him squat down beside a single red rose. He ran his fingers tenderly over the velvety petals several times before separating the flower from its stem. He held the flower to his nose, inhaling deeply. Finally, I asked him if this flower was special in some way. His eyes opened very slowly. "Every so often, someone breathes a prayer so pure and selfless, so full of faith and love that it just captures my heart." He stood motionless for an instant, then bent and buried the flower saying, "What glorious fruit this seed will bear."

We had been slowly making our way toward the opposite edge of the field when he stopped and turned back. He bent down, eyes flashing, and yanked an insignificant looking weed from among the brilliant red flowers I had passed through when I first entered the field. I followed the tendrils that trailed down from his fingers and back into the ground. As he pulled, I could see that they branched off in all directions and were entangling all of the plants in the surrounding area. His booming "*No!*" shriveled these invaders instantly and filled me with terror.

I drew back, fearing the raw power I felt emanating from him. He was clearly still angry when he turned back to face me, but I could also see such loving concern in his eyes. "The evil one seeks to entangle the fearful in his lies, hoping to choke off their prayers. But my father will not permit that!" He looked up, his lips moving, and I watched the strangled looking flowers plump up as fast as the tendrils retreated.

Nodding as if satisfied, he turned back toward me. Resting his hand on my back, he led me to a corner of the field completely covered with stately lily plants. "These are prayers for the gravely ill." Glancing about, I noticed that the ones in full bloom all had names seemingly embossed on them. "And *those* are prayers sent up by desperate relatives and friends for souls who died without having accepted salvation." I stood amazed, watching the name Emily Weller taking shape on the flower he held out to me.

"She died?" was all I could say.

"Not yet, but very soon. Your wife is praying faithfully for her, but so far she still resists." He again went down on one knee. Seeing a tear streak its way through the dirt on my friend's face, I struggled to make sense of his whisper. When he raised his face a few seconds later, I was astonished to see that his eyes were bright and peaceful once more. *Who was this man, and why would he care about crabby old Mrs. Weller?*

"Resists what?" The words were out of my mouth before an awareness, one I couldn't have put words to, began to take shape within me. As I stood, staring mutely at the ground, a single luminous, snow-white flower sprouted and blossomed at his feet. Something told me it was the key to this whole experience, so I looked to him for an explanation.

His whole demeanor seemed to change as he spoke. "That is the flower of life. It will bloom forever." I felt my gaze being drawn up to meet his eyes. "You're looking at it right now. I am the way, the truth, and the life." An almost unbearable longing rose in my heart. He pressed the flower into my hand. "Drink deeply of me and become a warrior in my Father's Kingdom."

I stood staring into his eyes, unwilling to look away, until at last he draped his arm across my shoulders. "It's getting late; let's go inside and get that cold drink."

Looking over my shoulder in the gathering dark, I saw the field once again smothered in flowers. Seeing my wide eyes, he laughed, "Yeah, I know. My Father's work is never done."

"Can we talk some more about that prayer warrior thing?"

He smiled, "I'd like that."

If my people, who are called by my name, will humble themselves and pray and seek my face and turn from their wicked ways, then I will hear from heaven, and I will forgive their sin and will heal their land. 2 Chronicles 7:14

Then Jesus told his disciples a parable to show them that they should always pray and not give up. Luke 18:1

Do not be anxious about anything, but in every situation, by prayer and petition, with thanksgiving, present your requests to God. Philippians 4:6

Rejoice always, pray continually, give thanks in all circumstances; for this is God's will for you in Christ Jesus. 1 Thessalonians 5:16–18

Devote yourselves to prayer, being watchful and thankful. Colossians 4:2

Every Created Thing

The wonder of trees bowing down to Jesus came to me during a Bible study years ago. Scholars have long debated whether images like those given in Psalm 148 can be taken literally. I don't claim to have the definitive answer. However, the propriety of every created thing raising itself to passionate worship, each according to its nature, resonates so strongly with my spirit that I felt compelled to *attempt* to capture how that might look. Perhaps this is fantasy, but what a lovely thing to contemplate.

I see majestic oaks bowing low to honor their maker. Their leaves sweep the ground. Then, straightening together, the trees raise their gargantuan branches heavenward, waving them about gracefully. The wind rushing through their leaves scatters the clouds into ever-changing patterns.

Grasses shiver with delight. Straining upward to catch the breeze, they whisper a soothing song of praise. They twist their blades, individually and in unison, to capture and softly reflect his magnificent light.

Mountains rumble a deep chorus. Their rocks clack and tock a joyful rhythm. Pebbles fling themselves blissfully down from the heights, landing then leaping delightedly back into the air as they tumble down the mountainside and settle peacefully wherever they land.

Waters honor him in the manner of their course. Rivers roar God's energy and power yet never overshadow his restful peace as made known through the gurgling of the smallest brook and stream.

Stars twinkle and flash a lovely show across the velvety blackness of the endless night sky. The moon shines quietly, peacefully content merely to reflect his glory. Meteors shoot blazing trails, celebrating the vast expanse of God's created universe.

Flying insects dart and flit in a buzzing dance of ecstasy, effortlessly in tune with the trill and chirp of songbirds. Creeping creatures slither and scratch, as they are able, in humble reverence for their maker.

Prey seeks predator, approaching unafraid. Nose to nose they meet, exploring and extolling the wonders of our Lord's creation. Until at last, as ordained before the dawn of time, they lie down together in eternal, peaceful harmony.

Some of the Pharisees in the crowd said to Jesus, "Teacher, rebuke your disciples!" I tell you," he replied, "if they keep quiet, the stones will cry out." Luke 19:39–40

You will go out in joy and be led forth in peace; the mountains and hills will burst into song before you, and all the trees of the field will clap their hands. Isaiah 55:12

Let the sea resound, and everything in it, the world, and all who live in it. Let the rivers clap their hands, let the mountains sing together for joy; let them sing before the Lord, for he comes to judge the earth. He will judge the world in righteousness and the peoples with equity. Psalm 98:7–9

Praise him, all his angels; praise him, all his heavenly hosts. Praise him, sun and moon; praise him, all you shining stars. Praise him, you highest heavens and you waters above the skies. Let them praise the name of the Lord, for at his command they were cre-

ated, and he established them for ever and ever—he issued a decree that will never pass away. Praise the Lord from the earth, you great sea creatures and all ocean depths lightning and hail, snow and clouds, stormy winds that do his bidding you mountains and all hills, fruit trees and all cedars, wild animals and all cattle, small creatures and flying birds.
Psalm 148:2–10

Each New Day

God created all things, and without his sustaining hand all of creation would unravel. Therefore, whether we recognize it or not, He is *always* at work. I ask God to open the eyes of your spirit to see him in this imaginary predawn ritual.

He watches over his children as they slumber, tenderly restoring frail bodies and healing broken hearts even as he prepares the new day—a day he planned before the dawn of time.

He warms the sun and freshens the air while steadying planets and brightening stars.

He smooths the sky and shapes some clouds, breathing out a gentle breeze and releasing his refreshing rain.

He paints the flowers and sets some to bloom. He rehearses his songbirds while dressing the trees.

He fills the seas and caps his mountains afresh with snow, all before re-counting the sparrows and the hairs on every beloved head.

Then, with divine anticipation, he touches each loved one individually, whispering, "Awake my love, and behold the day I have prepared. Come and sit with me for a while. Will you be my hands today?" To the willing among his flock, further guidance is given.

"Show him my forgiveness."
"It is time to tell her the Good News."
"Tell them I'm near."

When our awesome God gives us another day, let us live it in joy and profound gratitude. Let us stop often to take in the unmatched beauty so evident even this fallen world. Let us sing of his grace and peace. Finally, let us ever seek to bring our Savior's love and forgiveness to the lost and hurting among us.

The Spirit of God has made me; the breath of the Almighty gives me life. Job 33:4

For in him (God) we live, move and have our being... Acts 17:28

The LORD does whatever pleases him, in the heavens and on the earth, in the seas and all their depths. He makes clouds rise from the ends of the earth; he sends lightning with the rain and brings out the wind from his storehouses. Psalm 135:6–7

Sneak Preview of My Upcoming Book, "Should I"?

Is it really such a big deal for a committed Christian to become seriously involved with someone who does not share his or her beliefs? In four words, yes, yes, yes and *yes*! There may be times when it works well, but they are not the norm. Depending upon the personalities involved and how committed the Christian is, as well as how opposed to Christianity their partner is, the problems that *will* arise can range from mild to catastrophic. However, you can be certain that both parties will feel the impact.

In my experience, the believing partner in a long-term, unequally yoked relationship must continuously choose between staying in sync with their unbelieving partner and an active growing relationship with Jesus and his church. Either alternative requires the believer to marginalize one of them at least to some degree. Maintaining a close, dynamic relationship with Jesus is always challenging while living with a nonbeliever, simply because they will not share the Christian's enthusiasm for the things of God's Kingdom.

Trying to find, and maintain, a balance between the above options feels like walking a tightrope. Whom do I please in this minute, Jesus or my loved one? Make no mistake, loving and honoring your partner pleases Jesus. However, having to focus on maintaining your balance is exhausting and not extremely productive. Not only is it unfulfilling, but it also leads to resentment in both parties. I will be the first to admit that attempts to please someone from a place of bitterness are anything *but* pleasing.

As is probably obvious even this early on, my goal is to give my readers things to consider *before* they enter into a romantic relationship with an unbeliever. However, the situation is entirely different for people, like me, who are already married when they come to know Jesus. The Bible clearly instructs those of us in that position to stay in our relationship and to put in the effort to honor our non-Christian spouse while *still* following hard after God.

If any brother has a wife who is not a believer and she is willing to live with him, he must not divorce her. And if a woman has a husband who is not a believer and he is willing to live with her, she must not divorce him. 1 Corinthians 7:12–13

Being in an unequally yoked relationship is God's will for me in this season, and, although it is sometimes incredibly hard, I believe he will give me grace day by day to do it. However, if you are not already in a relationship with someone who does not love the Lord, the Bible repeatedly warns against putting yourself in that position.

Do not plant two kinds of seed in your vineyard; if you do, not only the crops you plant but also the fruit of the vineyard will be defiled. Do not plow with an ox and a donkey yoked together. Deuteronomy 22:9–10

As I write this, I have been married for forty-one years. Unfortunately, for thirteen of those years, my husband and I have been looking at the world through decidedly different glasses. Where I see God's wondrously intricate and thoughtful design, he sees merely random chance. I see God as my creator, my Lord, my Father, my protector, my companion, my healer, and my counselor. He sees God, "if he even exists," as a sort of absentee landlord.

My husband is annoyed by my belief in heaven and hell, and with my assertion that the choice we make today about Jesus is the single most important one we will ever make. We can't, (and to be honest, we really don't want to) see the world through each other's lenses. That makes for a lonely and frustrating life for both of us.

Scripture often uses the yoke symbolically to illustrate putting together two things that are similar in capacity so that they can work together successfully. It was common for a farmer to use either donkeys or oxen in cultivating the ground, placing the plow yoke on either two oxen or two donkeys. It is also common knowledge that the physical anatomy of the ox's neck and shoulder muscles makes it stronger than the donkey and more suited for bearing and dragging the plow. Even so, that does not necessarily make the ox faster. Therefore, placing an ox and a donkey together under the same yoke would be unfair. Disregarding the differences in build, nature and temperament produces inconsistent performance and results in decided discomfort for both animals.

Similarly, God commands Christians not to marry unbelievers because he knows it opens them to discomfort and disharmony. What they and their spouses treasure most in life will likely not be the same. What they see as life-giving is often quite different. They may even find they are not on the same page morally. They may have differing principles regarding childrearing. These differences exist in all marriages, but they are exaggerated in unequally yoked relationships because the people march to different drummers.

It is important to note that unequally yoked couples will feel the ramifications of that choice on more than one level. There are, of course, the everyday frustrations encountered when people with different perspectives on what is acceptable, desirable, and important try to walk together. For the Christian, though, there are also the deeper problems and pain that come with loving a person who believes this life is all there is. The unbeliever's focus during this life will naturally be different from that of a person who looks toward the eternal.

Then there is the biggie, that is, the anguish of living with the knowledge that your sweetheart continues, year after year, to choose eternal damnation (however unknowingly) over the presence of their wise and loving creator.

For the Christian, the struggle is twofold: how do I learn to honor God and overcome my "self" (self-righteousness, self-centeredness, and all the other "self" states I tend to dwell in) so that I am able to love my non-believing partner well, exactly as they are *today*? At the same time, how do I attain wholeness and remain in a balanced, healthy state myself while living in this incredibly lonely and frustrating situation?

In an unequally yoked relationship, at least one of the non-Christian's struggles is to understand that their partner's love for Jesus need not threaten them. They are not in competition with Jesus. He is God, and they are their partner's earthly love. If the relationship is to succeed, they must accept that while Jesus is the center of their loved one's world, the Christian's desire to become like him, will, in ultimately, make him or her a better partner. Finally, they need to realize that blessing their Christian partner's love of the Lord does not mean they will be required to "join the club. That choice is entirely and eternally theirs to make."

About the Author

Sharon Sekerak is a retired systems analyst for the Department of Defense. She lives in Cleveland, Ohio with her husband of forty plus years and is the mother of two amazing adults. Since leaving public service in 2009, Sharon has kept busy with volunteer work at her church, where she also leads a women's bible study. She enjoys spending time with family and friends and feels incredibly blessed to be able to combine two of her favorite things, her love of God and writing.

Although *What Our Lord Can Do* is Sharon's first published book, she has three others in the works. Each is decidedly different, but they all are aimed at displaying the beauty, wisdom, and power of our God as well as the tactics of our enemy, the devil.

CPSIA information can be obtained
at www.ICGtesting.com
Printed in the USA
BVHW081727130120
569392BV00003B/379/P